From Dreaming the Dream to Sailing Away: Buying the Perfect Boat

15 Steps to Buy Your Perfect Cruising Vessel and Sail Away

Steve H. Steakley

Captains' Admiral Publishing

Steve Steakley

ISBN-13: 978-0-692-81649-3

ISBN-10: 0692816496

Edited by Lia Steakley Dicker

Photo Credits:

Cover photo and vision board photo

by Admiral Lynn Steakley

Author/editor photo and Captain/Admiral photo

by Skipper Russell Dicker

Library of Congress Control Number: 2017908083

Captains' Admiral Publishing: Austin, Texas

Steve Steakley

This book is dedicated to my wife,

Admiral Lynn,

who kept safety above all else and

kept me out of jail.

CONTENTS

Subscribe and read the boating publications that cater to the type of sailing you are interested in, whether it is racing, weekending, coastal cruising, or ocean voyaging. Check out yachworld.com and let your fantasy run free.

Estimate in terms of size of boats that you will include in your search and a maximum you are willing to pay.

List every boat that catches your eye. The spreadsheet will develop over time as you begin to understand the characteristics in a boat that are most important to your planned use.

We went through two brokers before we found one who actually listened to us and was always available and patient enough to work with us for over two years.

This will narrow down the list.

ACKNOWLEDGMENTS

I want to thank the global sailing community for their contributions to the art, science, and adventure that created sailing and formed what is today in the twenty-first century. Whether it is day sailing or racing on an inland body of water, coastal racing, coastal cruising, ocean racing, or ocean passages across the world, sailors all collectively benefit from the adventures and design of this vast community.

On a more personal level, I thank my former brother-in-law, Thomas Logan, and his family for allowing us to share their Chris Craft Cherokee 32' sailboat *Bartom* on Eagle Mountain Lake in North Texas, where my own interest in sailing was born. Much later, the fine members of Hill Country Yacht Club at Canyon Lake in Central Texas helped me and my wife relearn to sail on our Catalina 250 sailboat *Moon Chaser*. They taught us how to race, go on a weekend cruise, and charter boats in the Virgin Islands. Two mentors were instrumental in our early development as sailors: Derek Crawford, who shared the secrets of racing, and Charlie Teat, who not only encouraged the racing but also led the charter trips to the Virgin Islands. Jerry and Melanie House, Greg and Katie Williams, and Derek and Judy Crawford became like family during our charter trips to the British Virgin Islands and to Belize.

I would also like to thank our Commander's Point Marina friends on Lake Travis, who continued the learning curve with us. We were often sailing on the lake with Pat and Bill on their Pearson 33 *Alchemy* on our respective vessels, and the "race" was always on. Dr. Ken Dorman on his Dana 24 *Star* constantly reminded us "life is way to short so better sail now." I am grateful to Paul Coburn, the Harbor Master, aboard his Pearson 39 SV *Papalota*, who taught me more than a thing or two about boat maintenance and restoration; Rick Johnson, aboard his Catalina 34 SV *God Speed*, who shared boat project solutions and life in the "Fjord"; and Buzz and Terry, aboard their Pearson 35, who made the trip to the Pacific Northwest to help us sail our newly purchased "most perfect" boat to Port Townsend for decommissioning and preparation to get it ready for its transport back to Texas.

I'm forever grateful for Kent Little, our yacht broker in Kemah, Texas, and surveyors Alain Vilage in the Pacific Northwest and Mike Firestone on the Texas Gulf Coast, who all gave first-rate service and helped us learn the art of buying and maintaining boats. Many thanks also to Daryl Gatewood of Gatewood's Service and Repair, Don Glandt of Gulf Steam Marine, Lisa Vizzini of Port Townsend Rigging, and Matthew Sebring of Coastal Bend Yacht Services for providing the top-notch professional services in our quest to ensure our cruising yacht was safe and seaworthy, as well as educating us improving our boat-owner skills. The second owners of our vessel, Barb and Josh Wallace, on board their Heritage East 36 MV *Last Trade*, not only contacted us first but spent time helping us to learn all about our new vessel and then became part of our ever-growing community on the Texas Gulf Coast.

Jake and Jenny Jackson, aboard their Endeavour 40 SV *Honky Voodoo*, introduced us to Corpus Christi Bay and the Bay Yacht Club. The members of BYC provided invaluable coastal cruising guidance. Bill and Pam Carrothers, aboard their Passport 42 SV *Wave Dancer*, not only introduced us to coastal cruising and beyond but also provided my first ocean voyage experience across the mighty Gulf of Mexico as crew on a rip-roaring five-day passage to Pensacola, Florida.

I thank the entire crew of the Erickson 36.2 SV *Apotheker* with Captain Jim Clower and First Mate Phillip Austin, who invited me along on two of their races from Galveston to Port Aransas, Texas, in the annual Harvest Moon Regatta. It was another whole set of invaluable experiences with this motley crew, and I had the privilege of crewing when *Apotheker* placed third in class.

The "dockmates" (an all-inclusive term for those who provide help when you need it and party till the party is over) and others you meet along the way provide support that go way beyond common friendships. Wendy and Randy Bond, aboard their Cruise-A-Home 40 MV *Bout Time*;

Ernie and Linda Glick, aboard their Catalina 30 SV *Salty Paws*; Cap't Woody and Pat Wood aboard their Morgan 41 Out Islander; and Mark Babcock, aboard the Morgan 38 SV *Take Off Time* (who helped us straighten out a mess after a racing collision), are the best dockmates you can ask for.

The Great American Loop Association and their members we met along our cruise around the Gulf Coast and Southeast Atlantic coast of Florida provide lots of local support, dock parties, and camaraderie that only cruisers know too well. Thanks to Bill Wilson, aboard his Morgan 33 SV *Breezin*, who served as first mate on the return trip to St. Petersburg, Florida from Marathon, Florida; John Furlinger, onboard his 1979 CYS 44 SV *Fairwind*; and Maureen Stotland, aboard her Allied Princess 36 SV *C-Lover*, for crewing on the best seven-day passage across the Gulf of Mexico anyone could hope for. It helps to have crew aboard that knows more than you do so there is always a learning curve.

Most of all my wife, Admiral Lynn, who took this journey with me one step at a time. Her mission was always that we arrived safely at our destination whether it was a two-hour sail on the lake or a long cruise down the coast. She was also our tour guide, making sure we saw it all before we departed to the next destination.

I

INTRODUCTION

Our own search for the perfect ocean cruising sailboat sets the tone, content, and spirit of this book. Since we are sailors, this book emphasizes the sailing side of buying the "perfect vessel" experience. The ideas of organizing for a "objective approach" to boat buying is applicable to all types of vessels, and I feel that whether your dream includes, a power yacht, a trawler, or even a river barge, you will find this book helpful in realizing your dream. There is a popular saying that goes "The best two days of your life are when you buy a boat and when you sell it!" If you have not already heard the comment, you will hear the refrain over and over again in your boating life. Dr. Ken once said, "shopping for a boat is the most fun part of buying." Especially since you somehow find time to step on and "pull the shrouds," so to speak, of lots of different vessels in the hunt to find *the boat*. The sentiment is absolutely true from my experience. Buying boats is fun. Selling the boat is also one of the best days, as it provides funds to start all over again and hunt for the next boat.

In our early twenties, my wife and I would crew/race on my brother-in-laws' family sailboat, a Chris Craft Cherokee 32 SV *Bartom*. We would always make a weekend of it, and when I wasn't on the water, I'd peruse the sailing magazines lying about their lake house. More than anything else, it was these publications that were filled with stories of sailing off into the sunset to uninhabited beaches of uncanny beauty that planted the seed for my dream for cruising on a sailboat. I stored those adventurous tales securely in my long-term memory until the kids were grown and we could sail away.

Years later, as we neared our fifties, I began to think again about a sailboat. My first thought was to buy a sailboat that we could trailer and travel around to different lakes or bays as we relearned to sail. The trailerable Catalina 22 sailboat spoke to me. We could spend weekends on it and experience lots of different water environments in the search for a future homeport. I found a used C22 on Lake Travis near Austin, Texas, and took my wife, Lynn, to see the boat. After viewing the fine little vessel, she looked at me with that *look* and shook her head and said her primitive camping days were over; better find something a little bigger. Did she say bigger? Heck yeah!

Our first sailboat was a 1999 Catalina 250 *Moon Chaser* that we sailed for four years on Canyon Lake near New Braunfels, Texas. We joined the folksy Canyon Lake Yacht Club and enjoyed the benefits of having a large community of very nice boaters both power and sail, to teach us how to race, charter in the Virgin Islands, and get the most out of our little boat. It was the nine-day trip in the beautiful British Virgin Islands with two other couples on a Jeanneau 46 sailboat that reactivated the dream to someday do this on our own vessel. The Admiral remarked how beautiful these environments were and the only way to experience them was by boat!

We later decided to buy a bigger boat and put her in waters closer to our home in Austin, Texas. I planned on a twenty-eight-foot boat, but after doing a little shopping, the Admiral again said, " I think you need to get a bigger boat if you really want to go cruising some day." She was absolutely right this time. So we bought a 1986 Catalina 30 (C30) sailboat. It had all the big-boat systems on it, including an inboard diesel engine, air conditioning, refrigerated icebox, galley with pressure water faucet and sink, head, and holding tanks—plus leaks! The very supportive Catalina Owners Association was a big plus in continuing with the Catalina design. The C30 owners' website forum helped us get our boat ship-shape and in *Bristol* fashion in just three short years.

It was not the sailboats, the racing, or all the other fun we had with our new friends on the lakes but going to the islands with them and chartering forty-five-foot boats to sail around beautiful blue water and incredible islands that convinced me that I truly wanted to spend as many retirement years as possible on a big boat, wandering around. That little seed sown in the early 1970s on Eagle Mountain Lake began to grow into a full-blown dream.

When I was not sailing, I was reading everything I could find about sailing, cruising, navigation, electronics, and maintenance or repair of boats. I subscribed to a variety sailing magazines for years and read them all cover to cover. As all boat owners know, you can't find the "everything" boat, and you have to figure out how you're going to use it and write a prescription to fill the need. I found www.yachtworld.com is a great place to cruise all the possibilities and vicariously explore all kinds of fantasies.

We had owned our C30 for two years, and retirement was coming for us soon. I began the search for our perfect cruising boat. The 1986 C30 was a great school in boat repair and restoration so I knew I could find a boat that was structurally sound and complete any necessary restoration myself, allowing us to buy more boat for the money. But it had to be the *right* boat. We could not afford to make an error in choice, as it could be costly in both money and time. I started by creating a spreadsheet. Using the data on yachtworld.com, I added over sixty different cruising style yachts to the spreadsheet and quickly began to gain an insight to the characteristics that would be desirable and those that would not be desirable in a blue water-cruising sailboat. I began to sort the boats and created a top-ten list. As I learned more about ocean cruiser sailboat design, I would move those that did not meet our *prescription* to the bottom of the list and note the reason why.

We were fortunate to live near the Houston-Clear Lake area, where the third-largest collection of recreational vessels in the United States are moored, sold, and traded. Lynn and I began to make regular weekend trips to Kemah, where we put our broker Kent Little through the long search for a boat that would meet our specifications: it had to be between thirty-eight and forty-four feet long. This all had to do with space and what I believed would be the limit in the practical size of boat a retiring baby-boomer couple could handle in terms of both size and budget. I am not sure how many boats we stepped on, but we continued going to Kemah periodically for two years, putting Kent through the paces.

I read two books that helped to narrow the list to a top ten: *The Complete Guide to Cruising Boats*, by Marshall and *Sailboat Design I & II*, by Robert Perry. Certain design ratios became the centerpiece on my spreadsheet for comparison as I realized the ratios facilitated a more objective approach. On one of our latter visits to Kemah, we were over by the Higgens, Smyth, and Hood brokerage docks and we were leaving after spending a few hours looking at a couple of boats. As we were walking back to our cars, Kent stopped on the docks and said, "You know I just sold this boat to this couple and it might be what you are looking for. I know the couple would not mind if we stepped aboard and take a look." I immediately declined since the boat was not on the list, but Lynn said she wanted to see it, so we interrupted the retired Coast Guard captain and his admiral. They were very nice, and we spent ten or so minutes aboard looking around. I really did not want to interrupt someone who had just bought their dreamboat so I cut our visit short. But when we got back to Austin, I started researching the Endeavour 42 Center Cockpit. It made our top-ten list.

If you are reading this, then you are most likely looking for your second, third, or even fourth boat. First-time boaters are rarely in search of their *dream vessel*. Instead, they merely want a safe boat that can provide the type of recreation they are after whether it is racing, cruising, or just getting away from it all. The focus of this book is on finding the *most perfect* dream cruising vessel, but if you are after the perfect racing or cruiser/racer, there is plenty of substance here to guide you to a increasing objective approach to turn your dream into reality and help you avoid a few of the pitfalls that could turn the dream into a nightmare. If you are just beginning to think about boating, then the following *precursor* is for you. Throughout the book, I will include what we did, the lessons we learned, and suggestions for a better plan.

Our search for the perfect boat took about three years, but I started organizing the search almost four years before we planned to buy the boat. This is a common pastime of boat owners to get on the Internet or walk the docks to check out bigger boats. Well into our search, I realized our vessel needed to fit *our* needs, including the physical abilities of a couple of physically fit, postretirement baby boomers living on our teachers' pension. I have organized our particular process to fifteen different categories. The focus of the approach is on how to move from your dream to sailing away. The foundation of the process is comprised of our time spent on the water and our experience buying a used fiberglass sloop, blue water-cruising vessel. After reading several other how-to books on buying boats, I knew there was something missing that I could contribute. Know that your solution will be different, and remember the hunt is fun—so make it last.

Please note that this is not the complete guide to buying a boat. I do not claim to know everything about the process because it is largely dependent on your specific dream. I have left what I have not stated for you to write about as soon as you can, preferably before I go to the "big ocean in the sky." I want to know a little more before that time. If the *complete guide* book were actually available, it would save us all a lot of time and money. Even if it were priced at $10,000 a copy, it would be well worth the price!

As a bonus, I have included a chapter on selling your *perfect vessel* when that time comes. It very recently came for us as a move to the Pacific Northwest dictated the need to sell *Wand'rin Star* and find a new vessel in Puget Sound. The learning curve never ends for sailors, whether it is sailing or buying and selling.

II

PRECURSOR: BUYING YOUR FIRST BOAT AND JOINING A BOATING ASSOCIATION

What comes first—the yacht club or the yacht?

In our case, we bought a boat that was a short walk down the dock to the front door of the yacht club. At the time, the dues at the Hill Country Yacht Club on Canyon Lake, Texas, were about $27 per month, and they were actively recruiting new members. This gave us immediate access to a wide knowledge base that would support our every move as we learned to sail, race, and even charter larger boats. The best part was the lake and the yacht club were only about an hour's drive away from our home in Austin. Having the boat close by meant we could go every weekend if we wanted to.

Below are some important questions to consider in the first boat-purchasing process:

1. What experiences do you have on the water?

2. How long have you been boating? What is your sailing or powerboating experience?

3. How do you intend to use your first boat? Day sailing? Racing? Lake or bay cruising?

4. Do you want to participate in weekend bay or coastal cruising with groups? Or, do you want to participate in club racing and be able to weekend cruise occasionally with the same vessel?

5. Where will you keep the boat? In a marina wet slip, at the marina on a trailer, or at home or storage lot on a trailer?

6. How close is the nearest body of water where you could begin your boating experience?

7. Is there a boating association near your home or the place where you plan to boat?

Any experience on the water counts! All water activities are precursors to owning your own vessel, starting with being a competent swimmer. While there have been more than a few boat owners who swim like a lead brick, you will definitely enjoy your boat more if you are not afraid of water. The skills you use in the greater variety of water sports will directly translate to your developing sailing skills.

How long you have been boating is less important than how often. The person who manages to get out just once a month has only four to a dozen experiences over the course of the year. The weekender may squeeze out somewhere between sixteen and fifty experiences. The person who lives in a year-round boating environment and can get to the water with just a short drive a couple of times after work may be well ahead with 150 – 200 experiences within a year. Of course, all this is determined by many factors, with weather and length of boating season having the greatest effect. Many regions have year-round boating, while others may have less than six months.

If you have a competitive nature, then racing may be a fun way to explore sailing—especially since the learning curve is steep and fast. Do you like to take weekend trips to new destinations? Then trailer sailing may be a good option for you, and there are associations that will support those adventures allowing you to sail in a variety of environments, both inland and coastal.

Yacht clubs, boating clubs, and sailing or boating associations come in a wide variety of missions and purpose. The range in yacht club or boating association dues and commitments varies from as low as $12 annual dues to those offering a five-star dinner club to finish your boating day off. Regardless of the price and club amenities, any boating organization will assist you in learning all about the type of boating your interested in and shorten the learning curve, leading you to enjoy a progressively more challenging and fun environments in the safest way possible.

Let's just say, for example, that you have a competitive side and sailboat racing appeals to your sense of adventure. Your best bet would be to visit the nearby organizations that promote and organize sailboat races. Give them a call, look them up online, and go check them out in person. If they race one-design fleets, then that may be the boat for you to start out on. Often a club member has a boat for sale and the vessel probably has a history with the club, so it is easy to get started with the help of other members. If a competitive environment is not in your blood, then consider buying an inexpensive day sailor to sail on a nearby lake or bay to hone your skills. Go to the nearest coastal bay, and take a sailing course from the American Sailing Association (ASA) or United States Sailing Association (USSA). Watch the YouTube video "The Physics of Sailing" at www.youtube.com/watch?v=yqwb4HIrORM. This video is excellent at explaining the forces that act on a sailboat that allows you to sail both downwind or upwind.

There is no way to dream without a vision. If you have not already owned a boat, then it is time to jump in the water. Many would suggest you first get some boater education. One option is to take an online boater safety course. Several states offer free or affordably priced online courses. My advice is to buy a boat and get started. More formal class work can happen after you find your first boat. If you own a boat, then you are twice as motivated to get training and you do not have to wait after you complete your coursework to put your new knowledge to use. Just get in the boat and start slow. The chances of you scratching or banging up your boat are high in your first learning experiences so that is why you do not want to spend a lot of money on your first vessel. Fiberglass is pretty forgiving and easily repaired. Be sure you and your crew wear life jackets!

Some choices to consider:

1. Trailer Sailor (18-23 feet in length): If it is a sailboat, I suggest that it has at least two sails, a jib, and a main, such as a sloop otherwise known as a macroni rig. You can make do with an open cockpit and a boom tent, but those with a small cabin that sleeps two allow you to weekend

on them (out of the rain) and camp out on the lake or bay. They have a porta-potty and sometimes a small galley on board, and this would be a great way to explore lakes and bays in your state. Here is just one website that can get you started http://www.trailersailors.info/. Expect to pay $2,000 to $5,000. Not hard to find deals!

2. Pocket Cruiser (22-26 feet in length): A pocket cruiser could be pulled with a trailer but is a lot more convenient to leave them either on the trailer in a marina or in a wet slip. Pocket cruisers often have a small galley with a one- or two-burner stovetop, an icebox, and a small sink. Boats in the twenty-four to twenty-six feet range will have a porta-potty in an enclosed head. Expect to pay $3,000–$10,000 for used vessels but remember this is just a beginning so keep it closer to $5,000. Visit http://pocketcruiserguide.com/Over20Feet.htm for more details.

3. Racer/Cruiser (28 to more than 35 feet in length): These boats are great for club racing and weekending. They are called PHRF (Performance Handicap Racing Fleet) racers, and a handicap is applied for racing to account for differences in design. Racer/cruisers are great for club racing and cruising since they have a galley, refrigeration, a full head, and sleeping accommodations.

4. One-design race sailboat (12 to more than 30 feet in length): Search for the nearest sailing or yacht club that supports one-design racing. Often these are inexpensive clubs with less than $50 monthly dues. Go hang out with them and find out how to get involved. Often you can just join and find a boat to crew on. It's much better to buy your own boat since this learning curve is where you want to be. Often boats are available from club members who are selling and moving on to the next level. One example is the J24 fleets, which are seen all over the world. You can find a J24 for around $4,000 or less. It may have worn-out sails or a few other issues, but it is a way to get started and the sailors around you will help you get the boat into competitive shape. It is not about winning at this stage anyway. It is about learning.

To us our twenty-five-foot sailboat was a big boat. Think of your first boat as a small yacht. Any experience on the water will pay off big returns as you move to your next boat. As soon as possible, join a boating organization that offers a full calendar of activities for its members. You can always find these organizations online, and they are always recruiting new members. This is the best way to maximize the fun of learning all aspects of boating. The benefits of joining local yacht clubs include a wide range of other water activities. Many form groups to go on bareboat charter trips to beautiful destinations all over the world. And they always get preferred group rates that are hard to beat. One example is sailing for singles clubs, and there may be one in your area. Visit http://www.singlesonsailboats.org/ for more information.

Sailing clubs or boating clubs could be a nonprofit type or for-profit type. Both offer a broad selection of boating activities and are often good options for people with very little time for maintaining and owning a boat. They have either affordable charter fees or a low monthly flat fee, allowing you to reserve your vessel in advance and hop on and go. The clubs do all the vessel maintenance and pay the moorage fees.

The benefits of clubs include plenty of local-knowledge experience, outreach to future chartering experiences, and boating education including ASA Certification or USSA certifications. You can often find either a ASA or a USSA school available at nearby inland lake; however, I strongly recommend that you make the effort to take these courses in a coastal environment. Everything they teach you will apply to inland waters, but the experience on the water in larger bodies of water will whet your appetite for more. Also you will get to practice in areas where there are many more navigation experiences of all types, which helps to boost your learning curve. Soon after we bought our first boat, I arranged for us plus our adult son to go down to Corpus Christi Bay and take the ASA course on Basic Keelboat Certification. We all had a great time, and the course, although unknown to me at the time, prepared us for our first trip to the Virgin Islands on a bareboat charter trip hosted by the Hill Country Yacht Club.

Learning to do your own repair work and maintenance is also much easier with a support group like a club. There are many online "owners groups" that have online discussion boards where you can ask any question related to the vessel and you will get back several if not dozens of answers on how to resolve the issue. The Catalina 30 Owners group literally helped me learn how to fully restore our 1986 C30. After three years of puttering around on the boat, mixed in with lots of sailing, I had her fully restored and earned the confidence to move on to a larger vessel, knowing full well that I could tackle just about any kind of issue with the support of like boat owners just a click away.

It may be time to buy your next vessel when you have spent a few years on the water and feel confident and ready to move on to the next part of the dream. It may also be time to move to new waters where you can mix with a new group of boaters who have the next level of experience. If you spent the first several years of your boating life on an inland lake, I strongly advise moving your boating to a coastal area where you can dip into larger bodies of water like coastal bays that will eventually entice you to see what is beyond the cut leading out to the ocean. Big bodies of water like the Great Lakes certainly qualify since they have the same types of boating environments that you will find along coastal areas. However, if it takes a lot of travel time to get to the larger body of water, then it is not worth it if it prevents you from regularly being on your boat.

All the chapters in this book assume you have already owned one or more boats of any type either power or sail and that you have an interest in sailing away on an extended voyage on your own vessel some day. The dream is all-important, but at some point, if you are to move toward the reality of actually realizing your dream, then you need to begin to organize. Unless you organize, you won't be able to realize the dream. Boats are seductive. Each one is like a siren calling your name, offering its own fantasy of sailing away in its own fantastical way. In the same way you are attracted to another person, boats possess their own force of attraction. Fully recognizing the seductive nature of sailboats, I wanted to devise a way to logically pursue my dream. So I created an objective approach to avoid allowing my emotions to hijack the process. I think this approach will help you move from the sexy dream of sailing away to the practical reality of tossing the lines off the most perfect vessel for your adventure in the safest manner possible.

1
DREAMING THE DREAM

Those who dream of sailing away to far-away destinations come from every conceivable background. Most of these people wouldn't have ever met if it had not been for sharing the dream of getting rid of the majority of their material possessions and taking off on an adventure across bodies of waters large and small. Everyone out there has a unique story with familiar threads. Each dream is so distinctive that it creates a one-of-a-kind experience for the dreamers. If two sailors sail the same exact route, they will have completely different experiences with only a few similarities. The one thing in common that links all these adventurers together is the water and a vessel. The way they found solutions to their journey to life on a boat seems to have more differences than similarities.

Dreaming about boating should include all of your senses. I once read that sensing is done at primitive levels in the cells and integrated into sensations in the nervous system. So use your sight, smell, hearing, touch, and taste to visualize your dream of sailing through a beautiful body of water on the perfect vessel. Picture the perfect climate for your adventure. Hear the sounds of the wind in the sails and the boat charging through the waves. Feel the breeze on your face, the moist air on your skin, and the helm in your hands. Taste the salty spray in your face, and relish the smell of the fresh sea air. The dream is all-important. For without the dream, there would never be the reality of tossing off the lines and sailing away. Here are a few ways to nurture your dream.

1. Subscribe and read the boating magazines that cater to the type of boating you are interested in. The best things about dreams are they are dreams! Dreaming doesn't cost anything, and they are readily available. With a little imagination and prompting from outside sources, dreams can grow and be even more fantastic than ever. Some of the best fantasizing I have done is living vicariously through those who were

submitting articles to the various sailing magazines. I kept a running subscription to no less than five different publications at a time. My daughter once asked who was reading all those magazines. I was! *Sail* focused on racing plus other general interest. *Cruising World* provides the cruising side of sailing from coastal cruising to ocean passages. *Practical Sailor*, also known as the Consumers Report for sailors, rates all the latest products from chart plotters to the best wax. *Cruising Outpost* (previously *Latitudes and Attitudes*) provides tales of adventure, the party, and the fun side of sailing. *Good Old Boat* tells the story of those buying, restoring, and cruising the classics. There are many more publications to choose from both hardcopy and online magazines as well. Often there are local boating magazines that cater to a region like *Tell Tales* for the Texas Gulf Coast or *48 Degrees North* for the Puget Sound area. Search online for your specific interest, and you'll immediately find the appropriate publication.

2. No matter what your interest is, read Josh Slocum's book *Sailing Alone around the World*. Slocum's single-handed circumnavigation broke all kinds of barriers for all of us. Being the first man to solo around the world was no different from the first person to step on the moon. He demonstrated that a small wooden sailboat could safely navigate the world's oceans and thus opened up the possibility for the rest of us to follow:

I had resolved on a voyage around the world, and as the wind on the morning of April 24, 1895 was fair, at noon I weighed anchor, set sail, and filled away from Boston, where the Spray had been moored snugly all winter. The twelve o'clock whistles were blowing just as the sloop shot ahead under full sail. A short board was made up the harbor on the port tack, then coming about she stood to seaward, with her boom well off to port, and swung past the ferries with lively heels. A photographer on the outer pier of East Boston got a picture of her as she swept by, her flag at the peak throwing her folds clear. A thrilling pulse beat high in me. My step was light on deck in the crisp air. I felt there could be no turning back, and that I was engaging in an adventure the meaning of which I thoroughly understood.

Josh Slocum is every boater's hero even if they just day sail or motor along on a nearby lake.

3. Surf Amazon.com for publications related to your sailing interest. Try typing in the search terms "cruising boats," "racing sailboats," "sailboats," and "coastal cruising guide," and see what pops up. Amazon.com is a virtual library with even out-of-print books available. Your interest and your dream will easily choose the best titles to sink your teeth into.

4. Definitely surf www.yachtworld.com, the largest data bank of recreational vessels of all types for sale both used and new on the Internet. Do not limit your imagination here, and cast a wide net to see all the possibilities that exist in the world. In the search window select the following:

1. Use the advanced search option.

2. Leave the manufacture/model blank.

3.Select *all* for hull material.

4.Select *new* or *used*.

5.Select *all* for fuel.

6.Select *all* for engines.

7.Select the type: *all sail* for type of vessel.

8. Select a minimum and maximum for length

9.Leave the year blank

10.Enter *zero* for your minimum price and choose a maximum desired for price. This is dreaming. Even if your budget is $100,000, expand the budget, for dreaming purposes, to make it $300,000 or more and get a feel for the market. It cost nothing to dream.

11.Select your desired unit feet or meters.

12.Select your type of currency.

13.Select *all* regions of the world to view different types of vessels that may not be available in your home country but are on the market in other parts of the world. The selection is really amazing to see.

14.Check the box at the bottom to exclude fractional boats. These are boats being sold to a group of people who would share ownership, expenses, and time on the boat, much like time share vacation properties.

You will be surprised at how many sailing vessels you find with twin engines. And, of course, you get to consider catamarans—do not rule them out. Your search will provide vessels of all types, and by browsing through the pictures and specifications of the individual vessels, you will soon learn a lot more about your dream. A good friend told me the best part of boat buying is the search. Let your fantasy run free.

But how long should you stay in this fantasy stage? Stay as long as it takes to get all your senses fully involved. The dream will become much more defined, and you may already be hatching a few preliminary plans to test your dream out a little further. Dreaming for me started in full swing after owning our second boat for about two years. We had an invite from some friends at Canyon Lake to go on a bare boat charter to Belize aboard a Fontain Pajot 46 Catamaran. The waters of Belize are much more primitive than the US and British Virgin Islands. We all had an incredible lifetime experience sailing inside the reef, and it firmly established our desire to buy a cruising sailboat. After our Belize adventure, we came back to Texas and made arrangements to take the next series of ASA certification classes, Bareboat Chartering, and Basic Coastal Cruising on a four-day cruise to Galveston Bay destinations.

If you have been sailing in a nearby inland lake, consider making the move to the coast. One caution here is that if the coast is a long drive from home, it will put a severe pinch on the amount of time you spend on the water. Time on the water is more important than driving long distances in a car. You can always get coastal experience by occasionally chartering a boat in a coastal location. We were getting hungry to charter a boat on our own. So we went back to where we earned our ASA certificates on Galveston Bay and chartered a thirty-four-foot O'Day for a full-day sail. The experience was one more link in the chain. Armed with a whole new learning curve, I spent the next two years on yachtworld.com and reading books directly related to our more well-defined dream.

Let's hit pause for a moment. I feel that at this point I should offer a word to the wise as you begin this journey. The number of couples cruising around the globe is pretty amazing. And I have always wondered what the real ratio is of successful to unsuccessful cruising couples. Part of this curiosity stems from our time cruising in South Florida where we met men single-handedly cruising on all types and sizes of vessels. I wanted my mate and admiral to take this journey with me, so I made sure to break it down to small chunks of learning where she was there with me every step of the way. It's much better to have her learn alongside in the same coursework, environment, and teachers than to have me serve as her primary teacher. It is not easy teaching family members since your expectations are high, emotions can rule, and your patience is certainly not in balance with the endeavor. We have seen way too many skippers bark commands at their mate in harsh tones. Each time this happens, it continues to drive a wedge between the skipper and admiral, which ultimately results in either a sale of the vessel or the skipper sailing alone. So if your intent is to bring your mate on this journey, then be sure to take small manageable steps in order not to overwhelm your partner. It is much easier and better to make sure all the crew receives training in a healthy, nonthreatening environment so that the result is enjoyable and leaves everyone eager to continue learning.

2

ESTIMATE VESSEL SIZE AND BUDGET

Now that your dream is full blown, it is time to add a dose of practicality. In most cases, some estimation of a boat budget starts taking shape. In our case, I started out with $150,000 as a total budget for all costs associated with buying the boat. I guesstimated around $100,000 to $120,000 for the boat and another $30,000 to $50,000 for the rest of the cost. These could be any of the following:

1. Haul out and yard bill expenses

2. Survey

3. Shipping cost if you have to have the boat trucked or sailed to your homeport

4. Upgrade cost such as electronics. Some brand new vessels do not come with all the modern-day electronics like chartplotter, DSC/VHF radio, depth, speed and wind instruments, or cruising essentials like AIS, radar, and SSB radio

5. Initial marina or moorage cost

6. State registration, taxes, and federal documentation

7. Boat insurance

8. A few boat bucks for good measure. When we owned our first two boats, a boat buck equaled $100. For anything over thirty-three feet to about forty-six feet, a boat buck equals $1,000. You will have to ask those who own bigger boats what a boat buck equals. I do not even want to know! There comes a point where if you have to ask then you can't afford it. It is often said that "B-O-A-T stands for Break Out Another Thousand."

The first boat we bought was relatively new and a broker was not involved. We made a deal with the owner and kept the marina slip the boat was already in. There was no surveyor and, we incurred none of the above expenses except for state registration and sales tax. We didn't know any better, but it worked out for us. The boat was only three years old, and the previous owner had not done any upgrades (like drill holes). The above-listed eight items were based on the experience we had with our second boat. We bought the boat in Kemah, Texas, from a brokerage and had to have it trucked to Lake Travis, which of course involved most of the above. By the time planning came around for our cruising vessel, we had some idea of the possible hidden costs.

Somewhere I read that couples cruising in and around the world were doing so on the average of a forty-foot (40') vessel. So I narrowed the search limits from 38' to 44'. Interior space, storage, and especially tankage were important to us. Anything under 38' usually had small fuel and water tanks. Once you break the 40' size, the costs of parts, maintenance, repair, insurance, and moorage really start to climb. It was actually frightening to think buying a boat much bigger than 40' because of what I estimated as the available cruising budget we might be able to sustain. The other piece was the ability for two baby-boomer retired teachers to manage a vessel any larger than 40'. We met a couple in their seventies who had been cruising for nearly fifteen years on a eighty-foot Gulfstar. They brought their boat to the Corpus Christi Boat Show to try and sell her. When I spoke with the owner, I told him I was amazed two people were able to manage such a large vessel. He said with hydraulic winches and steering that it was as easy as a 40' boat. But the budget to maintain and operate her was certainly three times a 40' vessel for sure!

Many live the cruising dream on vessels far smaller than 40'; it depends on your needs and vision. When we were in Marathon, Florida, at Boot Key Harbor there was a single guy on a small 1980s 26' single 50-hp outboard cabin cruiser. He traveled down from the Northeast on the

AICW, and he told me he paid $500 for the whole rig! On the other side of us was a $2-million-dollar 78' motor yacht. Yet there we all were in the same destination enjoying the same slice of paradise and experiencing the dream our own way. It was at that point that I came to the full realization that it truly is not about the size of the vessel you own, but it is about the journey. No matter what size boat or budget is, you can share the same environments and destinations. So estimate the range in terms of size of boats that you will include in your continued research and a maximum you are willing to pay. Next refine your search on yachtworld.com and keep dreaming.

Narrow the range in terms of length that you will include in your search. If you have reason, narrow the year range. I was not interested in any vessel made before about 1985. Through my dreaming on yachtworld.com, I noticed there appeared to be a significant design change around that year and I seemed to gravitate toward vessels built in 1986 and or later. A lot of this also depends on your budget. We purchased our cruising boat in 2008, and 38' to 44' vessels from 1986 to 1991 were typically within our budget. I knew there would be compromises and I would have to step up and resolve them. But our experience restoring the 1986 Catalina 30 gave me confidence.

Narrow the maximum you are willing to pay, and continue to set the minimum to zero. Because you never know when someone wants to quickly sell a boat they are not using anymore and lists it significantly below market value.

Narrow the hull type, and if you're interested in more than one type of hull material, then do separate dream searches. Make a list of characteristics or features that you must have and would like to have if possible or do not want in the vessel. For example, we wanted at least a 50-hp diesel auxiliary, two separate cabins, lots of tankage for fuel and water, and preferred a cutter rig.

3
MAKE BOAT COMPARISON EASY AND CREATE A SPREADSHEET

The spreadsheet should list first those features that you
1. Must have
2. Desire or would like to have
3. Do not want

The following is an example from our spreadsheet:

Requirements:	Blue Water Off Shore Boat	
Adequate space for extended live aboard/cruise for couple with occasional guest		
Minimum 38' - Max 42'	Prefer 12' + Beam	
Cutter Rig		
Master / guest staterooms	Not interested in 3 cabin layouts (ie charter type boats)	
2 heads, 1 w/Separate Shower Stall		
Outfitted for cruising	Interested in Pilot House/ hard dodger	
Marine AC/Heat		
Full or Modified Full Keel	Skeg hung Rudder	
Draft not > 6'		
Full dodger/Bimini		
Adequate Anchor Rode	Adequate Windlass	
Full Batton Main	Roller Furling Headsails	
Depth/speed/Wind Instr.		
Minimum 40+ HP engine	2 x gross weight=desired HP	
Heavy Displacement >20,000 pounds	Capsize Ratio<2	
Want to avoid lots of exterior wood & old screwed in Teak decks		

The primary purpose of the spreadsheet is to objectively organize each vessel's characteristics and make it easy to compare boats. The following list is a snapshot. It is the result of a lot of online browsing on yachtworld.com and reading numerous sailing articles and books. Our most perfect boat now had a skeleton, but there were a lot of cells to fill in. List every boat that catches your fancy on the spreadsheet. The full list will develop over time as you begin to understand the attributes in a boat that are most important to your planned use. We had over fifty different boats listed on our spreadsheet after the initial online research. We would add fifteen to twenty more through other means such as weekend trips to Kemah to shop boats or being invited aboard others vessels either as crew or guest.

Here is an example of a beginning worksheet with the top-section vessels researched on yachtworld.com or other online sources

Boat Manufacturer	LOA	Draft	Keel	Displacement	Beam	Eng HP	Separate Shower	Heads	Stateroom	2nd Stateroom V=Forward V Berth	Yr.	Asking $ Low	Asking High$
Albin Nimbus **	42	5'-10	skeg/modified	23,325	12'-6	44	yes	2	Aft	V	81	71,000	97,500
Brewer Aft cockpit CT	42	5'-3	Modified/Skeg	32,000	13'-6	84	yes	2	Forward-v	Aft Quarter Double	87	128,900	149,900
Brewer Center Cockpit /CT *	42	5'-3	Modified/Skeg	32,000	13'-6	84		2	Aft	V	87	139,900	
Brewer Pilot CT	40	5	Modified/Skeg	23,000	12'-6	62	Yes-Forw	1	Forward-v	Port Pullman	88	109,900	125,000
Bristol-CC	41	4'-6/10	Modified/Skeg	26,530	12'-11	58	Yes	2	Aft	V	81	98,500	178,000
Aft cockpit	41	4'-6/10	Modified/Skeg	26,530	12'-11	52	Yes	2	Forward-v	Aft Quarter Double	89	165,000	215,000
Cheoy Lee Pilot House	43	5'-6	Full	34,000	13	120	Yes	2	Forward-v	Aft Quarter Double	81	169,000	
Cheoy Lee Golden Wave CT	42	6'-2	Modified/Skeg	25,090	12'-8	50	yes	1	Forward-v	Aft Quarter Double	84	135,000	
Sceptre-pilothouse	41	6'-1	Modified full	21,500	12'-8	55	yes	1	Forward-V	Aft Quarter Double	82	123,900	
Stevens Custom	40	6	Modified/skeg	24,000	12'-7	50	Yes	2	Aft	V	82	121,000	
Boats Stopped on/Researched													
Baba Panda	40	6	Full	29,000	12'-10	62	Yes	1	Aft	V	85	159,000	189,900
Baba Pilothouse	40	6	Full	29,000	12'-10	85	Yes	1	V-berth	Port Pullman	85	169,900	
Bayfield Ketch *	40	4'-11	Full	241,500	12	52	Yes	1	Aft/quarter	Aft/quarter	84	89,900	110,000
Endeavour-CC	42	5	Modified/skeg	25,000	13	50	Yes	2	Aft	Forward-V	89	90000	129000
Brewer Pilot CT	44	5	Modified/Skeg	23,000	12'-6	62	Yes-Forw	1	Forward-v	Port Pullman	88	115,000	144,900
Brewer Pilot/Center CT	40	5'-8	Modified/Skeg	23,000	12'-11	62	yes	2	Aft	Forward-v	88	120,000	

Data on the spreadsheet will quickly fill in and around the skeleton and you soon begin to bring the body into a clearer vision. There is still a lot of fun work to do as you construct a more objective perspective than merely a pretty boat. Add the column headings that are important to you. I will explain why I used the ones you see in this example.

Make/Manufacture: Occasionally a particular make of vessel is taken over by another builder, and so it is good to know who built the boat. For example, Catalina bought the hull molds and continued to build the Morgan 44 when Morgan went out of business. So they are now known as Catalina Morgan. Some manufactures had good years and not so good years. Hunter started out great, but had some low-grade builds in the 1990s. A new leader brought new life and confidence to the Hunter line in the 2000s. Valiant, a highly prized blue-water passage maker, had a few years where hull blisters were pervasive. I am sure second or third owners using new epoxy paint technologies have resolved most of these issues. This type of information is readily available on owners' associations websites.

LOA (length over all): Sometimes this includes the entire length of the vessel and sometimes not. For instance, if a vessel has a overhanging bowsprit, it may not be included in the listed length overall. One thing to keep in mind is that marinas will charge you for all overhangs in either direction when it comes to slip size, including a dingy hanging on davits off the stern. When we sailed our Endeavour 42 into Corpus Christi Marina, two guys jumped aboard with a one-hundred-foot tape and measured from the leading edge of the bow pulpit all the way to the end of the dingy hanging off of our dingy davits. So instead of paying for a 45' slip we paid for a 55' slip.

Draft: Draft is especially important in some waters, especially the coastal areas of the Gulf of Mexico Coast where it is wise to keep the draft near five feet. Note that vessels with center boards list two drafts. For example, a friend has a Irwin 47, and the draft with the center board up is five feet and with the centerboard fully down is nine feet. Some people avoid centerboard vessels due to complications of maintenance.

They serve a very useful purpose and can be the solution for making the transition from shallow sailing grounds to very deep water. Just know they require your periodic attention and may require some refurbishment every so often depending on how you use the vessel.

Keel: The type of keel is all-important when considering a vessel of any type. The keel greatly affects sailing characteristics and in some cases safety. Self-steering systems work better with longer keels. Narrow-fin keels and spade rudders may make it difficult for self-steering systems, especially in heavy weather. I was told that 80 percent of the vessels have bolt on keels; the other 20 percent are either encapsulated keels or some type of centerboard keels that allow one to navigate both shallow and deep waters.

Displacement: The rule for displacement, generally speaking, is you want light displacement for fast boats and heavy displacements for slower but safer vessels in ocean environments.

Beam: This has a lot to do with design ratios, stability, as well as interior space.

Engine Horsepower: It is generally recommended to have at least two times the displacement in horsepower. For instance, a 20,000-pound sailing vessel should have a 40-hp engine or higher. Our experience of chartering in the San Juan Islands with big tides of twelve feet or more resulted in very fast currents in narrow channels convinced us to go for the highest horsepower that was practical for the hull type.

Separate Shower: A lot of vessels have a combined head and shower. You basically are showering in the same space as the toilet. We wanted to have at least one separate shower unit so we would not always be soaking the entire head each time we took a shower.

Heads: We felt having a his and her head would be nice, but not essential. Also consider the maintenance of dealing with more than one head.

Stateroom: This has to do with the layout of the interior space. The choices range from having the owners cabin forward, amidships, or aft. I had this fantasy that occasionally either one of our adult children's family might join us for a week or so. This never happened. They were very busy leading their own lives. We loved our 42, but if I realized the reality before buying a boat, I would have been just as happy with a 38–40' vessel.

Second Stateroom: This means the second cabin space is in one of the other areas forward, amidships, or aft.

Year: We preferred 1986 or later due to some positive design changes after 1985 in the market. This is a personal choice and also has a lot to do with your budget. There are an amazing number of fifty- to –one-hundred-year-old wooden vessels sailing the waters of the Pacific Northwest in 2017.

High Listing Prices: While you would rarely pay the top asking price, even for a new vessel, it is good to understand the market so you can begin to develop a budget. Know that the market varies in different parts of the world. Used sailboats tend to go for higher prices in the West Coast than they do on the Gulf of Mexico Coast, and it, of course, has to do with regional economies and demand.

Low Listing Price: We all like lows, but beware! Vessels at the low end of price listings may have worn-out hulls, keels, rigging, or engines with hidden dangers. Or they might be some guy who has a really good value and needs to dump it to get out from under monthly boat payments, moorage fees, maintenance costs, and monthly insurance premiums. The monthly cost for a forty-foot vessel could be anywhere from $1,000 to $2,000 per month. If you are not using it, then it is best to sell quickly rather than to let it sit waiting for the perfect deal to come along. This is another reason why you need a qualified and trustworthy surveyor to help you close the deal.

There are several considerations when it comes to constructing your spreadsheet. Since it is easy to add or delete, add as many column headings as you feel are necessary to complete the framework around your dream. You can always outfit your boat with certain extras, such as electronics or solar panels, later. Patience pays off in the hunt, but at some point, you will step on a vessel and if she meets your fundamental criteria everything will fall into place. You will know her at that moment.

4
FIND A GOOD BROKER AND COMMIT

Sellers pay the broker, so why not use one? We went through two brokers before we found one who actually listened to us, was available, and proved patient enough to work with us for over two years. Most marinas have a brokerage office connected to them. If the office is not on site, then it is usually a short walk or drive away. When we went looking for our second boat, we started the search for the perfect twenty-eight-foot sailboat at the Kemah Boardwalk Marina. We perused the docks, saw a few boats for sale, and then walked into the onsite brokerage office. Mike met us as we walked in and we sat in his office briefly and described to him what we were after. We wanted a 27' to 28' boat to sail on Lake Travis near Austin as we continued on our learning curve as sailors. The first boat he showed us was a 44' Center Cockpit Morgan that was amazing to tour, but we were way overwhelmed and had absolutely no reason to even consider a vessel of this size at that point. When he took us below, the pungent smell of mildew overcame us so we kept our look brief. I can only imagine the owners finally got too old to sail her any longer and she was simply growing mold in the deepest reaches of her holds till either the right buyer came along or the price was reduced to entice a sacrificial lamb. Mike did show us a couple of 27' to 30' boats, but after two more weekends of him showing us mostly boats in the 36' to 40' range, we gave up on Mike. We went through one more experience like that and realized that a brokerage will tour you through their inventory first before showing you vessels listed with other brokers. But the process was not for naught. The experience gave us both a lot more knowledge of what we were dealing with as we ventured toward our next vessel.

The Admiral told me that if I really wanted to do the cruising thing some day, then I should consider a 30' boat to increase the learning curve. We had really enjoyed our little Catalina 250, and the owners association had been especially helpful when we wanted to do small upgrades or make minor repairs. We had a friend at Canyon Lake with a Catalina 30, and the Admiral liked it. So I traveled everywhere in Texas where there was a C30 for sale. I traveled to Corpus Christi, Port Aransas, Lake Texhoma, Lake Travis, and back again to Kemah.

One of the C30's for sale was at Sea Lake Yachts. Jerry and Melanie, friends at Canyon Lake who bought a Beneteau 32 through Sea Lake Yachts, recommended yacht broker Kent Little to us. Kent Little was our man. I explained to him the problems we had with previous brokers who showed things we had no business buying and of our hunt for the best 30' sailboat in Texas. Kent seemed to fit our style right away and was easygoing. He spent the day with us and showed us several boats 28' to 30' range, including several boats listed with other brokers and a C30 they had for sale. We were finally able to see several boats in our range with a knowledgeable broker and discuss the pros and cons. Kent recommend a surveyor, and we started down the brokerage path of boat buying. We were particularly interested in a 1986 C30 that had a brand-new 27-hp diesel, and there had been a recent survey by the same surveying office our broker had recommended. Since the survey just needed to be updated, a full survey would not be necessary and we managed to save a few coins. We drove down the next weekend for the survey and the haul out by the yard. A 30' sailboat does not look that big until you pull it out of the water. The survey and the sea trial with Captain Bill went so well that we closed the deal and arranged to have the boat transported to Lake Travis.

We learned tons by going through the process of dealing with a broker, surveyor, and Big John at the South Texas Boat Yard. Turns out that all three were doing their best to sell us that boat. We constantly had to try and read between the lines to try and stay even with them. The broker's office was across the parking lot from the boat yard and the surveyor just across the street. This was a very valuable lesson for us. This experience paid huge dividends in our dealings with similar characters when we bought our cruising boat later. The amount of money we may have overspent due to not being boat-buying savvy was chalked up to a valuable education and paid off for us when the stakes were much higher. We later learned that the brokers had a name for the inexperienced buyer: *novice*. The 1986 Catalina 30 was proclaimed the "hop boat" by the Admiral because it provided us the perfect classroom to learn how to restore and maintain a mini yacht, preparing us to hop to the perfect cruising boat.

Four years later, when we began the long hunt for our cruising boat, we returned to Kent and let him know we were beginning the process of searching for our cruising boat, but we were a couple of years out. Kent already knew what we were talking about and agreed to assist us in the hunt. His patience paid of for both of us.

5
STEP ON LOTS OF BOATS

We had a great advantage living close to Houston and Galveston Bay. Kemah, which is about a three-hour drive from our home in Austin, is located on Clear Lake and borders the northwestern side of Galveston Bay. Galveston Bay area is home to the third-largest collection of private recreational vessels in the nation. The majority of them are in huge marinas in and around Clear Lake, which has a channel to Galveston Bay. About three years into the ownership of our Catalina 30, I was a couple of years away from retirement and was ready to start the hunt for the perfect cruising boat.

We began taking weekend getaways to Kemah and scheduled time with our previous broker Kent Little. It was easy to research online the thousands of vessels for sale in the Galveston Bay area and make a list for each of the visits to Kemah. I would e-mail the list to Kent and he would make a few suggestions based on the list. We would take up an entire morning or afternoon on Saturday and Sunday and step on five to six boats. Pictures on the Internet are always dreamy, but stepping on the real vessel is sometimes a hard dose of reality. I would make notes along the way and come home and fine-tune my spreadsheet, moving some boats toward the top and others toward the bottom. This literally went on for nearly two years. It cost us mainly our time, but we turned the visits to fun mini-vacations.

This process will help narrow down the list as you become familiar with those aspects of boating you dream about. Always go back and add your newfound data to the spreadsheet. Make sure to list why you are eliminating a particular choice. Move it to the bottom of the list on the spreadsheet and create a rejected category. The result for us was a list of nearly seventy vessels, with ten rising to the top. You certainly do not need seventy vessels to compare, but I was having fun with the whole process. The cool thing is getting to see so many different solutions to the idea of building the safest and comfortable cruising vessel to get you to your destination quickly (think six knots for monohull sailboats) and stylishly (a perfectly subjective notion).

Being able to knock around the numerous possibilities with a knowledgeable and professional broker saved us from ourselves a few times. In one case, what appeared to be a great vessel was built in Taiwan during a period when only low-quality stainless steel was being used, resulting in rigging failures. In another case, where I was immediately taken by the craftsmanship of one vessel, I was informed the type of transmission it had was very problematic and costly to repair when needed. It was the only type of transmission that was available for this particular boat due to the way the engine was mounted. No, thank you!

We stepped on a worn and cruised out Passport 40. It was in such a bad shape that it sent shudders through my spine; I wanted to get off the boat immediately. The thought of buying such a boat that needed so much caused me to cross off the Passport 40 from my spreadsheet. Later a friend of mine bought one, and I had the chance to see it several times since it was in the same marina we used for a short time on Clear Lake in Kemah. It was flat-out beautiful, and I knew then that I had been way too harsh on my judgment about the boat. I had just stepped on a worn-out vessel that needed a total refit and it scared me! I was certainly willing to get a boat up to speed to go cruising, but I was not in it to completely refurbish a boat from top to bottom.

Reality soon begins to overtake the dream and certain features result in a top-ten list. Whether you are buying new or used, *value* becomes a key. Of course, you don't want to sacrifice safety or the other reasons for choosing a particular vessel. Some boats come with a lot more cruising goodies, electronics, or ready-to-go features. Remember, though, that it is the basic structural components of a boat that are of the utmost importance, so do not be swayed by a boat full of new electronics and other goodies. A few keel bolts with heavy corrosion or rust could spell a $5,000–$30,000 repair depending on the type of keel and the type of keel bolts. A top-ten list is useful for knowing that if any of the boats became available with the desired options already installed, then it may be the one. If you do not live near an area where there are lots of vessels to shop, consider planning a week-long vacation where you visit two or three different ports and get a reality check. If you have a broker you like, then talk to him about the possibility of co-brokering, where two brokers split the fee that the seller pays. You may not be able to take him with you, but he can call ahead for you to onsite brokers who will show you around and be equally interested in helping you narrow down your list. Having a broker that represents your interest relieves some of the pressure when working with salesman in far away communities.

6
EXPAND YOUR READING

As you begin to step on boats, this is the best time to start in on reading the *hard* material because you will be highly motivated by now to learn and understand every detail.

Start with the book *The Complete Guide to Choosing a Cruising Sailboat*, by Roger Marshall. The most difficult task is being "complete" about anything. Time and technology marches on. This book was copyrighted in 1999, and things have changed a bit since then. But the foundations remain the same when it comes to boating, so there is plenty to gain from Marshall. The next two reads get you a bit deeper into those foundations. Robert Perry's *Sailboat Design Volume I: 79 Contemporary Sailboat Designs Analyzed* really impressed me. After reading this book, I knew I was on the right track to limit the subjectivity of boat buying and put some real meat into insuring that we did not buy a work of art that would disintegrate in the middle of the ocean. Of course that whetted my appetite. I quickly consumed *Sailing Designs Volume II: 109 Contemporary Sailboats Analyzed* and the spreadsheet took on a whole new life, as I now included sail design ratios in the boat comparison.

 Next in line is John Vigor's *The Seaworthy Offshore Sailboat: A Guide to Essential Features, Gear, and Handling*. This book provides an honest look from an offshore sailor who has tested gear from the drawing room to the most serious of ocean environments. It would have been nice if I had read this one before we bought a boat. In chapter 2, he provides a way to evaluate boat design characteristics and score each one. The cumulative total determines the seaworthy ability of the vessel. His idea of "thinking inverted" as you go about evaluating the seaworthiness of a vessel is very valid indeed! I wished I had read it before we started stepping on boats, since I would have a much better perspective as we were shopping. "Preparation is the difference between adventure and disaster," says Marin Geogiev, chief petty officer for Princess Cruises.

Next you should read *How to Buy the Best Sailboat*, by Chuck Gustafson. On the back cover, it says it "covers every subject the boat buyer will have to deal with." Again I am here to break the news that one book will not be the everything boat book when it comes to all the decisions it takes to "buy the best boat." That being said, there is a lot of substance and it is worth the read. It will provide a lot of clues to what you may want to pay attention to. In my experience, the hunt, including all the reading, educated me with the tools I needed to make the right decision for us and that is what you are after.

Subscribe to *Practical Sailor*, which is the consumer report of sailing and will provide current technology product comparisons to refit and maintain boats of all kinds. I know several sailors who have years of back issues filed away for reference. You do not need them as time and technology have made most of them relics, and you can search all those topics on the Internet with up-to-date information. But *Practical Sailor* keeps you informed of the current technologies and which ones are worth your time and money.

A few more suggestions:

Rhonda Byrne's *The Secret*: Even though I had taught my high-school students to set goals and write out plans to achieve those goals, I never really went through the formality of all those steps such as writing sub-goals and committing to a date to achieve each step toward the desired goal. I was always successful using a calendar on my desk and writing out a short list to get through the day, week, or month. This book came along about the same time we were starting to dream of sailing away. I realized it was going to be a big challenge to just cut and run. We had spent over thirty years in the same house raising our two kids, spent most of our teaching careers in Austin, and our anchor was dug in deep. I read countless sailing articles of the stories where people sell their material belongings and the house to buy a boat. They sail away to paradise where they are the only vessel anchored in an incredibly beautiful island cove. The stories never wrote of the challenge of cutting all the ties and digging up the anchor that sank progressively deeper after years of moorage in the same town. *The Secret* gave me the inspiration and tools to commit to a goal and write out a plan to achieve it. I outline the plan in chapter 9. *The Secret* is about the laws of attraction, but I could not believe that I could just close my eyes, visualize what I want, and it would appear. I needed to be proactive. For me, a vision board helped center what I wanted and focus on the necessary steps to get us there.

Gregg Nestor's *Twenty Affordable Sailboats to Take You Anywhere* is a collection of mainly 1970s and 1980s vessels priced in the $20,000 to $70,000 range (in 2007 values). His book can give you some perspective of the market, and for those with a smaller budget, know that even after refit, they can come in at under $100,000. It's worth the read.

Bill Seifert and Daniel Spur's *Offshore Sailing: 200 Essential Passagemaking Tips* is definitely one I wish I read before sailing away. This man is extremely thorough. He covers the full gauntlet of outfitting a vessel for safe ocean crossings. All two hundred tips will not apply to every vessel, but I am surely glad I read it before I venture offshore again. I will make several improvements to insure we are safer than before.

As I was writing this book, I revisited the books I reference to fact-check and make sure my memory had not faded too much. I read two other books that are definitely worth mentioning here. The first is *A Sail of Two Idiots*, by Renee D. Petrillo. A couple of thoughts passed through my mind reading this book: don't be an idiot, and what doesn't kill you makes you stronger! I found myself aghast, amazed, I got mad at them, and then I forgave them along with many more emotions.

The second book is *Leap of Faith*, by Ed Robinson. I like Ed's verses on moving from a debt and credit home budget to one of debt-free and saving home budget. His chapter 20, "It's a Crazy World," is worth the purchase price alone; I laughed out loud all the way through that chapter. Also they do it on a trawler, so this one is for the power boaters for sure.

There are plenty of books available detailing the pros and cons of

1. The best type of rig for particular sailing purposes

2. The best type of keel

3. Going high-tech or keeping it simple

4. Lots of wood or no wood

5. Small versus large. It is interesting to see the list of vessels that have single-handed circumnavigated. Visit www.joshuaslocumsocietyintl.org/solo/solotable.htm

6. Type of hull material: There is a good reason the wide majority of vessels are constructed of fiberglass in the modern sailing era. Aluminum (think corrosion), steel (think rust), and wood (think rot and maintenance especially in warm waters) are all good choices for the right person, purpose, or the right environment.

7. Monohull, catamaran, or trimaran: I believe a lot of the old concerns have been resolved with modern catamaran designs. I really liked the Leopard 39 that was featured at the 2013 Miami Boat Show. It won the Boat of the Year award from *Cruising World* magazine in 2010. Several of the larger Leopards have won in the years since.

8. The region you plan on sailing. For example, if you want to sail in the North Atlantic, Pacific Northwest, or any other wet climate, a pilothouse or motor sailor may best fit your needs. For those who want to sail the Northwest Passage, steel may be your best hull material to defend against the ice.

9. How keel and rudder types affect self-steering in either electrically powered or wind-driven systems.

I know that by a wide majority the solution for most has been a monohull fiberglass hull, but that does not mean it is the best solution for you.

7
RESEARCH DESIGN RATIOS

There are a few design ratios that I researched and included information about on the spreadsheet. Understanding design ratios helps take the subjectivity out of the process and increases your chance of making a more objective decision. You will not buy a boat just because it is *beautiful*. There are many design ratios that yacht designers and builders pay attention to. I chose four of them to concentrate on when it came time to compare and choose our cruising sailboat. Once you learn and have a general understanding of these ratios, I recommend you add them to the spreadsheet for comparison values. In our case, I sort of threw a semi-educated dart. I assigned a value to each ratio that was preferred for *our* needs as coastal cruisers with a few ocean crossings expected. I am sure I erred on the side of safety. The numbers suggested below are for offshore, cruising sailboats.

I used Ted Brewer's website to help define the four design ratios that I explain below. Marshall, in his book *The Complete Guide to Choosing a Cruising Sailboat*, also covers these in detail. Several websites discuss these ratios in varying user-friendly applications. If any of these descriptions cause your eyes to cross, then do an Internet search for "sailboat design ratios" and choose a more readable version: www.tedbrewer.com/yachtdesign.html.

Here is another option—Ratios for Dummies:
www.mysailing.com.au/yaf-news/ratios-for-dummies

1. *Capsize ratio* or capsize screening formula (CSF) = $beam/(displacement/64.2)^{1/3}$ needs to be less than 2 for a cruising yacht. The CSF compares beam with displacement since excess beam contributes to capsize and heavy displacement reduces capsize vulnerability. The formula is the maximum beam divided by the cube root of the displacement in cubic feet: $B/Displ^{.333}$. The displacement in cubic feet can be found by dividing the displacement in pounds by 64. The boat is acceptable if the result of the calculation is 2.0 or less; the

$CSF \sim 2.15$ J97E

lower the better. A contemporary light displacement yacht, such as a Beneteau 311 (7,716 lb, 10'7" beam), has a CSF number of 2.14. Based on the formula, this vessel would be a fine option for a coastal cruiser, but such a yacht may not be the best choice for ocean passages. A note of caution using this ratio: any two sailboats will have the same CSF value if their displacement and beam are the same. For example, one could have a light hull with 50 percent ballast in a bulb at the bottom of an eight-foot fin keel, while the other could have a heavy hull with 20 percent ballast in a two-foot-deep (0.61 m) full-length keel. The stability characteristics of the two sailboats will be drastically different despite the identical CSF value.

2. *Displacement/length* (D/L) *ratio* should be > 280.   ⅃ 97E 204

D/L is displacement to waterline length (DLR) = displacement (lb) / 2240
$$\frac{\text{displacement (lb)} / 2240}{(0.01 \times \text{LWL (ft)})3}$$

The D/L ratio is derived from the displacement in tons (of 2240 lb) divided by .01 LWL cubed: $Dt/(.01 \text{ LWL})^3$. This ratio broadly indicates how heavily built a vessel is. Material is a key player in this ratio. The higher the number the greater weight for the given length and hence the construction is indicated as heavier. Very low numbers point toward racing. It is recommended you consider the D/L ratio when choosing a boat.

Boat-type D/L ratio for several types of boats are as follows:

- Light racing multihull—40—50
- Ultra light ocean racer—60–100
- Very light ocean racer—100–150   ?
- Light cruiser/racer—150–200
- Light cruising auxiliary—200–250
- Average cruising auxiliary—250–300
- Heavy cruising auxiliary—300–350
- Very heavy cruising auxiliary—350–400

3. Comfort ratio (CR) >30   *J97E*   *19.26*

The CR is displacement in pounds/ $(.65 \times (.7 \text{ LWL} + .3 \text{ LOA}) \times B^{1.333})$. Ratios will vary from 5.0 for a light day sailor to the high 60s for a super-heavy vessel. Moderate and successful ocean cruisers, such as the Valiant 40 and Whitby 42, will fall into the low-middle 30s range. The Passport 42's CR is 31.46 and the Catalina 400's is 23.61. I crewed aboard a Passport 42 during a five-day Gulf of Mexico crossing with several days of winds 30 mph+ and seas twelve to sixteen feet. Our buddy boat was a Catalina 400, and, by comparing notes with the crew of the Catalina, I can testify that these are much more than just numbers. The motion of the Passport, which was a much heavier vessel, drove through the waves, resulting in a much more comfortable ride. The lighter Catalina 400 rode on top of the waves, resulting in a very difficult motion for the crew.

4. *Sail area to displacement ratio* (SAD) < 19 for offshore cruisers.

Sail area with 100 percent foresail/$((\text{displacement}/64)^{.667})$ The sail area/displacement ratio is the sail area in square feet divided by the displacement in cubic feet to the two-thirds power, or SA/D$^{.667}$. This ratio is "nondimensional" and can be used to compare boats of different sizes. Mainly it is a "power to weight" ratio so that a boat with a higher value will accelerate better and be a better light air performer. It will reach hull speed with less wind and need to reduce sail sooner if it is to avoid being over canvassed in a blow.

Boat-type SAD for various vessels are as follows:

- Offshore cruisers—16–18
- Medium cruisers heavy—18–22
- Inshore cruisers, racing boats—22–26   *WTF??*
- Extreme racing boats—26–30+

J97 — 19?
(18.98)

J97E category is "racer"

Sailboat design ratio calculators

+ this works

This is Tom Dove's site that continues to provide Carl Adler's sail calculator on his website. All you have to do is choose the vessel you're interested in, and the numbers are calculated for you. You can even compare two vessels with a resulting chart. If the vessel is not listed, then you can forward the required numbers to Tom, and he will add the vessel to the list: www.tomdove.com/sailcalc/sailcalc.html

Or you can plug in your own numbers here, and the ratio will be calculated: www.ipass.net/sailboat/calratio.htm

For multihull use, www.multihulldynamics.com/

Below is an example of the sail design ratios data I included in my spreadsheet. When you have this picture in front of you, the comparison becomes much easier and you can be far more objective in your search for your "most perfect" boat.

Acceptable boats:	Capsize Ratio: Needs to be < 2	Comfort Ratio >30	Sail area Displacement <19	D/L Ratio >270	LOA
Caliber LRC	1.82	32.15	15.25	281	40
Endeavour-CC	1.78	34.98	14.55	307	42
Island Packet	1.83	32.21	15.24	267	38
Pacific Seacraft	1.72	36.82	16.27	349	40
Passport CT	1.86	31.46	17.57	265	42
Slocum CT	1.7	37.73	13.99	271	43
Vagabond	1.58	43.43	14.94	324	42
Valiant CT	1.73	33.96	15.51	256	40
Gulfstar	1.78	32.83	14.29	237	45

Note that the above table does not include the year model since it was taken from a larger spreadsheet. The year models we researched at the time typically included vessels between 1986 and 1991. A vessels design ratios can easily change over the years due to design changes. Be sure to do your own research for the model year and vessel you are considering.

J97E   L@WL/Beam is 2.42

"medium" is 2.7

8
SEEK TRAINING AND GAIN EXPERIENCE

You can't beat hands-on boating experience for preparing to go cruising. Included in that experience is learning how to repair or upgrade your own vessel when needed. If something breaks or fails, it often happens while underway, and if you are not close enough to the shore to call a tow, then you have to manage the issue. There are several options available for on-the-boat learning:

1. Join a boating association or yacht club. The combined experience of the members is invaluable. As is discussed in the precursor, yacht clubs and boating associations offer a wide spectrum of experience for free or inexpensive learning opportunities. When we moved to Seattle, I wanted to have the opportunity to sail in the Puget Sound waters; since our boat was in Texas, joining a sailing club was the most economical way of enjoying this experience. I was for the first time participating in a sailing club of this type. I joined Windworks Power and Sailing Club. where I met lots of sailors who had been members for years. They helped me with the local knowledge to safely navigate the waters around the area and also provided fun educational racing opportunities. Kristin Pederson, who is my supervisor where I volunteer to teach sailing and manages the adult sailing at the Center for Wooden Boats, also spoke highly of the advantages of belonging to a sailing club. Kristin said,

I'm glad you mentioned the recession in 2008–2009. This happened right when a lot of my peers were recently graduating from college, or fresh in the workplace starting their careers. I feel like it made us a bit gun shy, so to speak. To me, and I bet many of my peers would agree, the idea of buying and selling two to three largish boats seems too risky. Each one is an investment and there's no guarantee that it will be returned. There's no guarantee that investment accounts or pensions will be what they were in previous generations either, and I don't think you see younger people making as many larger purchases. I think it's more common to see younger people getting their experience through sailing clubs. I know you mention clubs as a good way to build a community and try out different boats, but I also know a lot of my friends who use that to gain extensive experience as well, and then when they're ready, they might go right to buying their "most perfect" boat.

Each generation leaves a formidable wake as they sail through life. The generation that follows has to navigate this new set of challenges. The rate of change is ever increasing, making the journey equally as intense. When the young dreamers arrive at their destination and they look across the horizons on the ocean of their reality, their experience will be balanced by their awe.

For many, the programs of sailing clubs provide much more than just day sailing, racing, or weekend cruising. The club provides lots of opportunities to experience several different types of vessels large and small and is extremely efficient in terms of money and time since these types of sailing clubs do all the maintenance, insurance, and slip fees. Members simply reserve their time, and the vessel they prefer is ready and waiting. During my one year at Windworks, I sailed at least eight different vessels ranging in size from 22' to 42' and participated in a very fun summer-racing series.

2. Crew with others on their boats and pick the owners' brain. I have been fairly aggressive about this one. I have had the opportunity to sail on at least fifty different sailboats and around ten different powerboats of all sizes from small sailboards to fifty-foot sailing vessels and small runabouts to forty-five-foot trawlers.

3. Boating in different types of environments is as important as crewing on various types of boats. We sailed on large and small inland lakes in Texas, coastal bays, the Gulf of Mexico, the Atlantic, the Caribbean, and Puget Sound. All of those experiences were invaluable to our learning curve. Salt water spells corrosion to almost everything except fiberglass, so learning how to keep corrosion and rot at bay is essential for coastal and ocean sailors.

4. Race whenever possible. Early on we raced our own boat. Later as we began to cruise, we continued to crew for others on all types of vessels from fast racers to PHRF cruising boats used for racing. Learning sail

trim means you can squeeze another knot of boat speed and a six-day crossing becomes a five-day crossing. Learning how to use currents to your advantage can also speed up a crossing. We sailed what on the chart looked like one hundred miles out of our way, but the advantage we gained in using the Gulf stream actually earned us more time resulting in a shorter passage.

5. Earn your ASA or USSA certification up to the bareboat charter level. ASA is a great association that promotes sailing of all types and is recognized throughout the world for their certification courses. It will provide you with the credentials required to bareboat charter. USSA does the same, and they are the sailing authority all the way through United States Olympic sailing. Charter when you can and look to find boats that may be on your prospective list. Chartering boats can be expensive. But if you find one or two other couples who would like to make the trip, then cost falls sharply. This is where boating clubs come into play and can really give you a lot for your dollar. We had the opportunity to go on four charters before we purchased our sailboat and one of the chartered boats, a forty-two-foot Tayana out of Bellingham, Washington, was on the top-ten list. I recently learned about NauticED from Kristin, which is an online interactive sailing education website: http://www.nauticed.org/. Kristin said, "They use online modules paired with practical experience to teach sailing. You earn badges online, and then validate them with the practical experience." One more but important bit of information I learned form Kristin was a website that offers online Safety at Sea seminars. I'm all for it; I am all about safety and being prepared. Here is the link: http://thesailingfoundation.org/what-we-do/safety-at-sea/

6. Making boat buddies on the dock is very valuable. They can help you when you need an extra hand, and helping them is like going to sailboat repair and maintenance school for free. The camaraderie that develops among sailors on the docks goes way beyond the next-door neighbor at home.

7. Join the owners online association. Most production boats have such an organization and some are more developed than others. Often the boat builders start up the organization as a way to promote their vessels. But it does not take long for the association to take up a life of its own and become the most valuable resource for the boat owners.

8. Consider a captain's license. There are online and classroom courses where you can study to earn a Coast Guard Merchant Marine license. I thought this would be especially valuable, as we wanted to navigate in ocean environments. Some of my sailing buddies did not think it was necessary to take the time to earn a captain's license. But as teachers we were accustomed to going back to school occasionally to update our skills or obtain new ones. Networking with others earning their captain's license led to a summer job driving boats on Lake Travis for Just For Fun, a company that chartered captained houseboats and party barges. The time on the water in a variety of vessels gave me enough sea time to qualify for my captain license. My friends were right that I did not need a captain license, but it added to my confidence level when it came to navigating across an ocean. Plus the summer experience as captain of party boats on Lake Travis taught me that I never want to be the person responsible for a boat load of partygoers ever again.

9. Crew finder websites are another possibility for identifying a wide range of sailing experiences. I considered this option but never went beyond surfing the many choices available. Two friends offered themselves up as crew and found that these experiences can be incredibly rewarding as well as not so wonderful. Do your research, and make sure you and the vessel are prepared for whatever crew opportunity you agree to.

(a) Findacrew.net provides recreational, professional, and commercial opportunities.

(b) Latitude38.com is an online magazine that has a crew list available for free.

(c) Pointseast.com is an online magazine with crew match list.

(d) Sailingnetworks.com is a free networking site for sailors that can be fun to explore while looking for opportunities.

(e) Sailopo.com's offshore passage opportunities requires a paid subscription. The paid-subscription benefit is intended to create a place where you can find safer opportunities. But you still need to do your own research and interviews to make sure the vessel and captain have the experience to go offshore.

(f) Crewseekers.net: Crew Seekers International is a paid subscription to connect amateur, professional crew, and captains for international voyages.

10. Volunteer opportunities. There may be some volunteer opportunities in your area where you can offer your time to assist with boating. In my case, I volunteered to be a Texas State Boating Instructor, and I taught the required Texas Safety Boating courses. I was the volunteer education coordinator for the Bay Yacht Club organizing monthly education seminars for the members. Later I found the Center for Wooden Boats at Lake Union in Seattle, Washington. Here I volunteer as a sailing instructor. The benefits have been all mine. I learned from my students to be an efficient and effective teacher, and the time on the water certainly enhanced my skills. Experience means sailing as often as possible in as many different settings or boats as possible. Make lots of sailing friends, and go out on their boats in their environments.

9

SEE THE VISION AND MAKE THE DREAM A REALITY

This chapter may only be of interest to a narrow group of readers. If you are an-about-to-retire couple and have a land anchor dug in deep, then our particular experience in cutting off the links of the land anchor chain one link at a time just may be helpful since you will have to consider and manage several of the same links.

After watching the movie *What the Bleep Do We Know* and reading the book *The Secret* during early 2008, I found myself with a few moments and wrote out a ten-step plan. I posted this plan on the bulletin board at my desk in the teacher's office area along with a picture of a forty-something-foot sailboat in a beautiful island setting. This was my vision board. I thought about it every day as I set about focusing on the things I needed to accomplish if I was ever going to really retire and buy the getaway boat. I included a date that I wanted to achieve each step as well. This is an important part of writing goals. You need to have the deadlines firmly stated in the vision, or else there is no real commitment to achieving the goal.

If you haven't already created a vision board, then this is the time to do it. Make your ten-step plan, and list the goals you need to achieve in your life to get to the point of owning the boat of your dreams. Perhaps you are already closer than you think and you only need a five-step-plan. Maybe you are a little further away and require fifteen-step-plan. Either way, consider the major steps you need to achieve to get from where you are now to actually sailing away.

Each of the steps will have some subgoals, but you can consider them as you are completing each step. Several steps may be in motion at the same time, and listing those priorities in smaller subgoals can help you stay focused on the end point. Buy a blank poster board, and search online for pictures that depict your personal dream or perhaps cutouts from cruising or boating magazines. Paste your pictures and ten-step-plan on the poster board, creating your vision board that you will visit everyday from now until completion. I had a divider wall that separated me from the other cubicles in our teacher's offices. I hung my vision board right in front of my desk, which kept the goal in the front of my mind. Every day I focused on completing the next step or subgoal. This kept me centered and on track to reach my goal deadlines. Words to the wise: watch out for what you envision because you will get what you want. After purchasing our perfect cruising boat, I put in over 372 hours working on refit and maintenance issues and about 95 hours installing upgrades. I haven't logged all the Admiral's hours of cleaning, searching for leaks, and all the other stuff she brings to my attention. It took me three years to get a thirty-foot boat back to new condition with modern electronics and so on when I was working full time. Our perfect cruising boat easily took that but with many more hours per year. The chances are high that you will do the one thing we were after, tossing off the lines. The real story of exiting an anchored land life and sailing away is detailed in the following list of how we severed the links off the chain and sailed away.

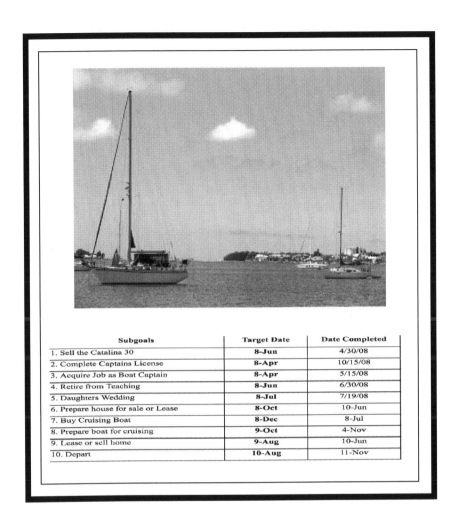

Subgoals	Target Date	Date Completed
1. Sell the Catalina 30	8-Jun	4/30/08
2. Complete Captains License	8-Apr	10/15/08
3. Acquire Job as Boat Captain	8-Apr	5/15/08
4. Retire from Teaching	8-Jun	6/30/08
5. Daughters Wedding	8-Jul	7/19/08
6. Prepare house for sale or Lease	8-Oct	10-Jun
7. Buy Cruising Boat	8-Dec	8-Jul
8. Prepare boat for cruising	9-Oct	4-Nov
9. Lease or sell home	9-Aug	10-Jun
10. Depart	10-Aug	11-Nov

Step 1: Sell the current boat. Target date: June 2008. Goal completed: April 2008. After a little over three years of owning our Catalina 30 *Hey You*, I put her up for sale using every free site on the web that my little search engine could find. After about eight months of showing the boat to many who just wanted to come out for a free boat tour, I finally got two serious potential buyers. A thirty-something tech guy from Dallas bought her and took her to Lake Texhoma. It is not always easy to sell what you have put your heart and soul into. I wanted to include in the contract that if he ever sold the boat that I would have first rights. The vision board helped considerably in getting past such trivial pursuits.

Step 2: Earn captain's license. Target date: April 15, 2008. Goal met: October 15, 2008. I was on the Internet checking out courses for what is known as the OUPV Six Pack Captains License. The nearest location to Austin to earn this license was in Houston. It would require three three-day weekends in Houston plus a testing date to take the course. This meant I would not only have the expense of the course but also have the hotel expenses. The six-pack license is what most charter sport fishing captains get since it limits the boat to six paid customers.

I wanted the license for two reasons. The first was to take the course for the knowledge to help me be a more competent and safe sailor. The second was to have the credential in case I needed to find paid boat work along the way in the event our retirement income was not enough to cover our cruising expenses. One night when I was close to committing to the course in Houston, I found a course coming to Lake Travis. A company, Just For Fun, had arranged an instructor to come to provide the course to several of their employees so they would not have to make the trip to Houston for the course. Serendipity! I was immediately sold since I would be able to easily get out to Lake Travis and avoid the travel to Houston and all the associated hotel expenses. I signed up that night with the Mariners School: www.marinerslearningsystem.com/home.php

Captain Richard Staggs was our instructor; he actually lived aboard his moderate displacement Mainship trawler in Kemah, Texas, and was responsible for conducting classes in Texas and Louisiana. The Mariners school has created a curriculum that has a high success rate for their students, and I highly recommend them if a captain's license is something you want to pursue. There were about fifteen people in the course from all over the state. This added to the course since there was a wide range of experiences to draw from. It is all classroom work. There is not any "on-the-water" instruction.

There are four basic modules you are instructed in and must prepare for comprehensive testing:

1. Navigation and rules of the road
2. Deck safety
3. Deck general
4. Piloting and general navigation

Once you begin to get into the curriculum, you realize this is not about sailing around the bay. The license is a US Coast Guard Merchant Marine License, and you learn things you need to know to go to work on a large merchant marine vessel. If you check out the above website, you can get more details on the curriculum. We took the exams, and all but one student passed all four tests. The navigation section was the toughest part since you had to plot out very specific navigation problems on a chart and provide your latitude/longitude answer. A small error with your pencil or straight edge would throw you off just enough to have to repeat the process two to three times. We were doing this in a classroom that was not moving. The tables were large and flat, and you could spread out the entire chart. Of course we had more than adequate lighting. I have yet to duplicate this on my own boat in a seaway where everything is moving and you don't always have the best lighting. We do chart out our course beforehand when the boat is in the slip and relatively still. We use a GPS chart plotter to guide us keeping the paper chart handy in the cockpit as a back up to our GPS navigation. The Admiral regularly marks the paper chart to update our position in the event our electronics die on us.

Of course the school is in it to turn a profit, so they offer certain upgrades to your license. Two of the upgrades that I was interested in were a sailing and a masters endorsement. I went to Houston to take the masters, sailing, and towing endorsement classes and exams. This was a three-day weekend, and this time, the students were more experienced and were from all over the southern United States. Passing the test does not get you the license. You have several more hoops to jump through; after all these are the USCG and federal government requirements.

Now that I had passed the academic requirements, it was time to get the physical part done. So a visit to the primary-care physician for a physical and eye exam had to be completed. When I presented the USCG form for the doctor's signature, she hesitated. The doctor scrutinized the form. Since she had given me a clean bill of health, I could not understand her hesitation to sign the form. I guess it must be due to all the litigation in the world. If I went out and had a disaster on a boat, then she would be the responsible physician who said I was in proper health to do the job. She signed the form, and off I went to the next hoop. Since our doctor did not have an audiologist in the office, I would be paying $100 out of pocket for my hearing exam. This I passed even though there are some frequencies/tones that I was deficient in (could be why sometimes I do not hear the Admiral). Next was updating my CPR certification. I found a class offered through the City of Austin. There were mostly fireman and other first responders in this class taught by a EMS Instructor. The EMS guy was the best instructor I ever had for CPR instruction, and it's not hard to imagine why. The last test is the drug and alcohol test. I saved this for last since I would be fasting from my favorite beverage a couple of weeks to make sure nothing would destroy all my efforts to get this done. Yes, I know alcohol washes out in a couple of days. But I was not going to gamble with all the effort. Five days later, I got the call that I was clean as a whistle. All that was left was to organize all my documents, make copies of them all, and find a weekday to drive back to Houston to turn it all in to the Coast Guards regional office.

I arrived around 1000 hours at the bland-looking office structure off one of Houston's giant freeways. I walked up a few flights and stepped into a small office where there were about five other guys waiting for their turn to be processed. The windows where the clerks were sitting were protected by very heavy glass that appeared to be bullet proof. Two guys went to the windows, the clerks asked them some questions regarding their paperwork, and they were sent away since they did not have everything in order. I was next. After several questions, the clerk made a copy of my documents even though I had made a complete set to turn in. She stamped everything and asked me to sit down. A few minutes went by, and another clerk opened a door and asked me to follow her. There were several employees on this side of the door in a huge office space. She asked me to raise my right hand and repeat the Merchant Mariner Oath. Here is where you find out that if the federal government ever needs your service then you have just given an oath to put yourself and/or your boat into the service of the military in time of war or disaster. About six weeks later, I got my fifty-ton masters license in the mail with my sailing endorsement. Hey wait: where was my towing endorsement? A quick call to the office in Houston and a coastie quickly identified the problem. He said it would be in the mail in a couple of days.

A reminder: Just because you have jumped through all the hoops to get the license does not mean you are ready to go across oceans. Only practical experience can prepare anyone for the task. We had a lot to learn, and we look forward to everyday spent on our boat in Corpus Christi for our next little adventure. One step at a time. I thought I would be able to make my deadline of April 15, 2008, but I really did not understand all the hoops you have to get through to get the license.

Step 3: Acquire a job as boat captain. Target date: April 15, 2008. Goal met: May 15, 2008. During the course, I met a group of people who worked for Just For Fun, a company at Lake Travis that rented boats of all sorts including party boats, house boats, and Sea Tow, which all required some level of captain experience. Since I needed additional sea time to qualify for the captain's license, I took a summer job at Just For Fun to acquire commercial experience. They were basically the only game in town for these types of services, so I worked as much as possible in all the opportunities they had. I worked with Sea Tow and towing boats that had broken down on the lake. I drove party barges all around the lake with a maximum of fifty passengers. I also drove a big

80' houseboat so I could qualify for the fifty-ton masters license. Since I had the Sea Tow experience, I could add the towing endorsement to my license. This was not the best summer for the Admiral since I was working a lot during the week days and all day and nights on weekends. The job at Just For Fun gave me the experience to qualify for a 50 Ton Inland Masters with sailing and towing endorsements.

Step 4: Retire from my teaching career. Target date: June 30, 2008. Goal completed on time. This would be the easiest step since I participated in a retire/rehire program four years earlier and went back to work at the same school while I waited for Lynn to retire. I finally threw in the towel and retired for a second time. Lynn decided to work one more year so this would give me the free time to work on all the other steps.

Step 5: Daughter's wedding. Target date: July 19, 2008. Goal completed on time. This was an incredibly important and exciting step. A return visit to Seattle and the San Juan Islands, where we had a fantastic experience a year earlier of chartering "KI" a 42' Tayana out of Bellingham, Washington, along with our daughter and future son-in-law as crew. They actually decided on Orcas Island for their wedding destination during the trip. Everything else was on hold until we passed through this wedding event. Well, almost everything. One of the boats we were interested in came up for sale in the Seattle area. I made arrangements to take the ferry over to Poulsbo, Washington, where I met a surveyor one afternoon. I thought, "What a stroke of luck! We could combine a serious look at a boat while we were in the area for my daughters wedding." The survey went well, and the wedding was *perfect*.

Step 6: Prepare house for lease or sell. Target date: October 2008. Goal met: June 2010. Holy Cow! Who would have guessed the almost Depression would happen right at this moment? We decided to move the target date out at least a year to see what was going to happen with the economy. We talked about our disappearing retirement investments and decided that Lynn would keep her job for one more year and that I would find work. I found a job as a CLASS case manager at the ultimate nonprofit in Travis County, The Arc of the Capital Area. I loved the job. I fit in like a glove with all my high-school special education experience.

After the hundreds of articles I have read about couples who sold everything and moved aboard their dream boat to go cruising, there was never a word about the transition of ending your day job and leaving your land-based home for over thirty years to living aboard a boat in a very humid location. The romantic articles would just say, "We sold all our stuff and sailed away!" As we neared the time to make a decision about either leasing or selling our home, we had already discarded a lot of stuff. There was a whole lot more to get accomplished if we were to actually dig up the anchor that had been buried for over thirty years and shove off.

First, there was the decision to sell or lease our home. Real-estate market conditions at the time, and a little fear of not having a backup plan in case all of this did not work as envisioned, held the cards. I remember reading an article in AARP magazine that encouraged their readers to keep their home for at least a year in the event that the move to their retirement destination did not work out. We were never the ones to throw all our eggs in one basket and take the associated risk that comes along with losing it all. My grandfather had a lot to do with the common-sense side of my particular attitude on all this; however, this was in direct conflict with my fathers' way of getting through the fog. He never hesitated to take off to California with twenty bucks, in a car with a half tank of gas, and no spare tire. He was resourceful and always got where he was going but lessons learned for sure. In the end, we decided to lease the house to make the Admiral feel secure in a bail-out plan. To prepare for either selling or leasing the house, I had already started and completed some remodeling projects.

The house we lived in for over thirty years needed bit more remodeling than we thought to get it ready to lease. We had completed some remodeling through the years, but it became clear that the old homestead needed more than we originally thought to get her ready to rent. The plan was to paint and put new flooring in the three bedrooms and the den area. All the other rooms were remodeled in recent years and seemed good to go. After meeting with Troy, who would be our broker and manage the house for 8 percent, gave us a few tips. First, idiot proof your home. Whoever moved in would not have the wherewithal or motivation to take care of anything so any new installation of items in the home had to be durable and simple to replace in the event they were damaged in the course of leasing to young, carefree, or careless tenets. Also as you begin to repair and make things new, other stuff jumps out at you and the remodeling becomes three times more the effort and expense than you originally thought.

When the construction crew came to fix all the cracks in the drywall, we thought we could stay in the home and hole up in our bedroom. We made it through, but that was a huge mistake. We should have moved out for a week and let them get it done. All those old trees had to go and new ones planted. The last thing we needed was a huge limb through the roof or falling on someone and having some kind of liability claim. It went on and on, and since we had signed a contract with the broker, we had to be ready to get out by July when most people are moving and leasing. About $12,000 later where I did most of the labor except for the drywall and roof part, the house was good to go. We hoped we could stay till August of 2010. Sure enough it leased, and we had to be out by June 30. We rented a condo in Austin for July to ease the transition to Corpus Christi.

Step 7: Buy boat. Target date: December 2008. Goal met: July 2008. Buying used boats is a major game event. You have to try your hardest to stay abreast of the brokers and everyone else who will profit from the sell of the boat. The seller is almost completely out of the picture. The only thing the buyer has going for them is their own research and the marine surveyor. But often these guys are great friends with the broker trying to sell you the boat, so you have to watch out for them as well. I got lucky and found the one surveyor in the entire Pacific

Northwest within a two-hundred-mile radius of Seattle that all the brokers disliked. He did a great job for us and helped to get the price down several thousand dollars. He pointed out lots of things that would need repair or replaced. Most of the items I could do myself. Plus, with the money he saved me, I could afford to have the rest of the project done by a yard once I got the boat back to Texas.

Step 8: Prepare boat for departure. Target date: June 2009. Goal met: October 2011. Well, of course, our lovely recession delayed this step. But the fact is you could work on a boat for forever getting it ready to go anywhere in the world safely. There are tons of articles of people positioned themselves in Florida and working on their boats to get ready to set sail, but never actually casting off the lines because there was always one more thing to get done first. There were two big-ticket items that we did not have on our boat: a water maker or a SSB transceiver, which are around $3,500 each. These items you only need if you leave the United States, so I figured that we could add them before taking off to the islands if that is what we chose to do.

Step 9: Lease/sell home. Target date: August 2009. Goal met: June 2010. No more mowing lawns! This was a huge part of the transition since we had to shed over thirty years of stuff. Thank you Salvation Army for bringing your truck! We still had a lot of stuff. Stuff we thought we would need for a while went into a 5×10 storage unit in Corpus Christi one car or truckload at a time. All the rest went into a 5×5 storage unit in Austin that was stacked up to the roof. We bought a lot of those plastic fifty-six-quart stackable storage containers at Home Depot to conveniently store the stuff. You never know what you may need. All but a couple of those containers sat in storage untouched. Right before we departed, we hauled most of it to the Salvation Army and put the rest on the boat.

The worst of my worries was changing our address and accounts including online accounts, investment accounts, and on and on to a mail service. No matter where we were we could call the mail service and have them forward our mail. I made a spreadsheet with approximately seventy-five different accounts to notify for address, phone, and e-mail changes. I wondered how do people who frequently move cope? I would tell techies I knew how they could become the next dot.com billionaires by simply coming up with a app where people could go and put in their old contact info and their new contact info and all their accounts would change overnight. This would of course include contacting all the government agencies as well. It is no wonder there is so much identity fraud going on. Everyone else is getting somebody else's mail. I had a spreadsheet listing all of our accounts, so I simply added a few columns and updated my progress checking them off as I changed the contact information.

The house was leased, belongings in storage, most of the address changes completed, and a condo rental in Austin for July. This gave us one more month to complete the transition to Corpus Christi. We had a retirement celebration planned for Lynn by taking a cruise to Alaska. It was a great diversion and a wonderful trip. We had an ace up our sleeve as we approached our move to the boat. We owned a small vacation rental with our son's family in Port Aransas, Texas. So if we needed a place off the water, we could always go there when it was not rented. This property proved to be a huge transition buffer. October brought great weather and we moved into a rhythm of coastal living.

Step 10: Depart. Target date: August 2010. Goal met with luck: November 2011. The transition to Corpus Christi was a far bigger deal than we thought it would be. We were living aboard our boat part time and spending the rest of our time at the rental condo in Port Aransas. But the condo was on the market and we hoped it would sell before November 2011. We spent the next year stretching our cruising legs around the South Texas Coastal Bend and continuing to outfit our boat for cruising and full-time live aboard. Living aboard the boat exposed some unforeseen problems. Certain boat systems do fine if they are used infrequently, but when you put them to the test 24-7, you find their weakness. We replaced one air-conditioning unit, a seawater pump, and the Adler Barber refrigeration unit for the icebox. It is best to have these corrected before ever leaving the dock for distant destinations.

Beware of Distractions

Keep in mind there will be distractions. Life is not seamless, and other things will take your time and money away from the goals you are trying to achieve. The trick is to minimize these distractions and keep your attention on the vision board and the dream.

The recession of 2008 completely sidetracked us. Anything regarding finances was no longer predictable and so we took a wait-and-see position. We were put on hold for just over a year when the economy tanked. We already had a steady retirement pension income starting to roll in, but the craziness of the world left us wondering if we would be able to sustain our path. We put it all on hold, and the Admiral kept her teaching job while I went back to work for a nonprofit. The one thing in the back of my mind though was the constant reminders from friends at Canyon Lake who were often ten years our senior and would say, "Don't wait!" over and over again. Meaning, do not wait to cast off the lines. Time is short, and if you wait too long, then you might be denied due to aging, health, family concerns, or other unforeseen events that prevent realizing the dream. After a year, we could see that we were not going to slide into oblivion and restarted the vision. We got into high gear, both leaving our jobs; leased the house; and moved aboard. Since I no longer had an office cubicle, I lost touch with my daily visit to the vision board. Staying focused on the vision board daily provided me with the discipline to strive toward the ten steps. The board would get lost under other stuff at home, and I would occasionally get it out and update my progress. I moved the steps to my computer, but instead of having them visually available, I would pull them up when I thought about it or to update the steps. Since I was successful in the first five steps and we were well along the way with steps six and seven, I felt like I had it down and was sort of on autopilot. I allowed a few distractions to encroach on the dream of sailing away.

The 16' Hobie Cat. This little distraction happened before we bought our Catalina 30. Before we got into sailing, we would take our summer vacations in Play Del Carmen, Mexico. The Admiral and I rented a Hobie on the beach and had a great time. When we returned home from that vacation, I soon bought a used Hobie that was missing a few parts. I found what I needed on eBay and enjoyed sailing this super fun boat on Canyon Lake and Lake Travis. I soon realized it was both a time and financial distraction from our goals. A young blood from the Dallas area bought it and took it to Lake Grapevine.

We joined the Bay Yacht Club when we moved to Corpus Christi. We knew the value of boating organizations and wanted the benefits of learning from their local knowledge as we learned to cruise around the Corpus Bay area. I became the secretary on the board of directors, and even though it was a valuable experience, it took our time and resources away from our goal of tossing off the lines and sailing away.

The most valuable lesson was returning to racing. The very first race with the BYC I put our cruising vessel in a situation that turned into a minor boat collision that took nine days of labor and $1,000 to correct. The Admiral said we should not be racing our cruising home! This experience brought me straight back to the vision board and from that point forward all of our sailing activities would support the vision.

Family either up or down. We are the baby boomers so we have children and grandchildren bringing up the rear and one set of parents still trucking through life. Family needs on either end can require your attention. One more reason to retire ASAP and get on with it!

We have a set of sailor friends who stopped working in their late thirties. They were both professionals with no children and saved a fine cruising budget. They bought a Shannon 37 and spent a couple of years outfitting the boat. They took off, sailed around Florida, and immediately headed for the Caribbean Islands. They sailed on their journey all the way to Trinidad and Tobago. They traced their steps back to the United States, cruised the East Coast, and after three years returned to their homeport in Galveston Bay. They sold the boat and returned to their professional lives. Their youthful health was excellent, and there were no demands from their family while they were away providing a relatively carefree experience. If you wait too late, health and family issues could keep you from tossing off the lines.

10
PREPARE A BOAT BUDGET (WHERE ONE-FOURTH REALITY MEETS THE DREAM)

Know exactly your financial limit, and save three times more money than you think you will need. This will leave a comfortable cushion for all the "unexpected cost" and keep the Admiral on board. In our case, I started out with $150,000 as a total budget for all costs associated with buying the boat. I estimated around $100,000–120,000 for the boat and another $30,000–50,000 for the rest of the cost like taxes, documentation and state registration, survey, decommission cost, recommission, boat transport, and any needed boat yard work like upgrades (think electronics).

Here is an example of our purchase cost for our Endeavour 42 center cockpit at 2008 prices:

1. Purchase Price:	$105,000
2. Coast Guard documentation and TX registration:	$792
3. Washington State Sales Taxes 6.6%:	$6,975
4. Dingy/OB:	$4,500
5. Survey $20 per linear foot:	$850
6. Decommission:	$1,659
7. Boat (truck) transport to Texas:	$6,500
8. Recommission (> 2× the decommission):	$4,895
9. Repair and upgrades at boat yard:	$5,728
	Total: $136,899

If you buy a boat near you and can sail it to the homeport, you can avoid three big expenses like decommission, transport, and recommission cost. The owner, outside of the vessel sale, sold the dingy to us. It was a brand-new dingy with motor, and he took a bit of a hit and we got a deal. We could have easily found a used dingy and motor for less, but new is always better. I calculated that the recommission and projects I wanted to get done at South Texas Yacht Services in Kemah would be around $3,000 or more, but it turned into a yard bill exceeding $10,000.

This is where I learned I could triple my expectations! We were still below our $150,000 limit, but in the next three years, we would spend $11,000 more getting the boat ready to depart.

Our total cost of the boat and upgrades to date is $140,597.17. After seven years of ownership, our restoration and maintenance portion is $36,506.45 to date. We lived aboard for five years and cruised two years. Other considerations, of course, include insurance and moorage. You want to have a good idea where you will turn for boat insurance. If you already own a boat, it will be a simple transfer of the policy to the next boat. The insurance company will require a copy of survey and will use the fair-market value of the survey to assign a value to the boat. This can be a little problematic when you add a lot of cruising gear and electronics and you want the total value insured. You have to pay for an updated survey, and the full cost of the added equipment usually does not raise the market value of the vessel to have the full investment insured. Then there is moorage. Often a marina will provide significant discounts if you pay for a year in advance. But this may not help those who are not planning on staying a year. So you will definitely have to pay the first and last months rent up front, which varies greatly due to location. A 40' vessel in a small marina in a small coastal town in Texas may be around $300 per month. But the same size slip on the East coast of Florida could easily be $1,000 a month or more.

Your budget will vary widely from our example above. One of my sailing buddies, Bill Wilson, asked me what the best boat was to go cruising on. As I paused searching for a short answer, he answered his own question: "The boat you own." He was absolutely profound in his insight to the reality of the cruising world. Every conceivable type of craft that floats either has, is, or will be used to cruise somewhere sometime. John Vigor, in his book *The Seaworthy Offshore Sailboat*, explains how one person took the boat he owned, a Catalina 27, and beefed it up in order to safely circumnavigate the world. The Catalina 27 was not built to be an offshore vessel, but this young sailor took the boat he owned and modified it to meet his needs.

11
NARROW THE LIST TO THE TOP TEN

Throughout this process, you will be refining your spreadsheet and moving the more desirable vessels toward the top and the less desirable vessels toward the bottom. Keep a running top ten and return to those often on yachtworld.com. Go to the yacht owners' website, and start asking questions to the owners of the vessels that interest you. A lot of the owners' sites have moved from an individual website to a Facebook page so consider searching Facebook. For example, the Endeavours owners site is www.endeavourowners.com/, but almost all the discussion has moved to their Facebook page.

Questions to ask current owners:
What do you like the most about your yacht?
What do you dislike the most? Or, if you could change one thing about your boat, what would it be?
What are common problems to look for?
What requires the most maintenance on your boat?
What improvement or upgrade was the most important?
What advice do you have for a new owner of this vessel?
If you had it to do over again, what would you buy? And why?
Where have you sailed the vessel?
What year and model offer the most value?
What are the sailing characteristics?
What are the anchoring characteristics?
How does the vessel respond in close quarters and docking?

While the true list of questions is infinite, these questions will kickstart the conversation. Boaters *love* to talk about their boats and are never bothered in any way by questions. If you are unable to find an owners' site on the web, then Google the vessel, and there is a good possibility that someone who owns a like vessel has a blog. Consider commenting on their blog to get contact information.

Reconsider any "must have," "would like to have," and "do not want" list. You are much more educated now on the practicality of what you consider essential and what can be compromised in search of the "most perfect" vessel. The features you gain with any "must-have" items are certainly trade-offs in another area. Dreaming usually denies the cost–benefit ratio of any feature on a boat, but practical use and safety can bring any desired feature into realistic perspective. One example is many prefer to have a rigid inflatable dingy, or otherwise known as a RIB. Storing a rigid dingy above deck brings certain risk in longer passages, and so having a simple inflatable dingy that can be rolled up and stored in a lazarette may offer the best solution for some.

Any of the vessels on our top-ten list could have been the "most perfect" boat under the right circumstances. They were all very similar in seaworthiness and size. Often a boat of the same make comes with a different engine size, interior layouts, and sail configurations so there are always choices to be made. Narrow down your list to the top three. Then visit your top three boats, even if you have to go out of state. Actually stepping on and closely examining your top vessels will help you focus.

When you find *the one*, notify your broker immediately. If the vessel is not in your local region, start the hunt for an independent surveyor in the area where the vessel is lying. It could well be worth it to provide transportation to a reliable surveyor if there is not one close by.

12
PREPARE YOUR FINANCING EARLY AND MONITOR THE MARKET

Now that you have done all the above, the rest of the process moves fairly quickly, and you need to be prepared if one of your top-three choices suddenly becomes available for a better than expected price. Our broker Kent called me and told me of a Vagabond 42 that would soon be available, and it was completely outfitted with a good price. I researched the vessel and knew it would be worth looking at, but we were not ready to buy. Buying early would put us in a time and money crunch that I was not willing to suffer. I told him we were several months out before being able to commit to a boat; he said that he did not think it would on the market very long. He was right; the boat was sold within thirty days. We took this as a sign that the vessel was not the right boat for us, and there were probably cosmic reasons for that.

Some sell the house and use the money for the boat, others have the cash, and another group find a way to borrow the money. We have never put all our eggs in one basket, as it is not in our character. But for others, it is the perfect solution. We discussed selling our home of over thirty years, but the Admiral did not feel comfortable taking off on such an adventure without having something to run to if we ran into the wrong hurricane or all the other things that one can imagine. No problem. I used a home-equity loan for the boat, which provided a few tax advantages. The federal government has been threatening for years in repealing the tax advantage of using a boat as a second home and disallowing one to itemize the interest from a boat loan as a deduction. They might accomplish that in today's political environment. So the home-equity loan works around that possibility. We leased our home, but we are fortunate to have a property in Austin, Texas where the real estate beats national averages. We have met people who found every conceivable way to sail away and if they needed funds they would stop somewhere and find work till the cruising kitty was restored. There are techies who still work full time but they do it from their boat, since the range of Internet access has dramatically increased through high-powered Wi-Fi systems.

All of this is to say that if you really want to accomplish your goal of sailing away, there is a way and you will find it. I am sure every boat broker has a willing and available lender to service your needs but as with anything shop for the best rates. Whatever your preferred solution, make sure to have a plan and be ready to go. If you have all the previous categories completed, then completing the purchase of the boat can progress quickly.

The Market Boat Value Guide is often used by brokers and surveyors is BUCValu and can be found at www.bucvalu.com/. This resource can help determine a close approximation to the value of different vessels, but know that different US or global regions could be plus or minus by thousands. For example, if a boat comes fully loaded with all the latest technology or cruising gear, this can result in a considerable price difference. However, it is rare for sellers to recoup the total dollar expense of having such gear added to the vessel. Buyers almost always get the advantage of buying a vessel already to go, and this can save many thousands for sure.

The following are some descriptors used to assist you in determining the value of the boat you are interested on Bucvalu.com.

Often Called	Description	Percent to be added or subtracted
Excellent (Bristol)	Maintained in mint or bristol fashion-usually better than factory new-and loaded with extras-a rarity	Plus 15-20%
Above BUC condition	Has had above average care and equipped with extra electrical and electronic gear	Plus 10-15%
BUC Condition	Ready for sale requiring no additional work and normally equipped for its size	No Adjustment Necessary
Fair	Requires usual maintenance to prepare for sale	Minus 10-20%
Poor	Substantial yard work required and devoid of extras	Minus 25-50%
Restorable	Enough of hull and engine exists to restore the boat to useable condition.	Minus 50-80%

In addition, the BucValu site has a Buc Appraisal form that you can print out and use as a checklist as you inspect a vessel to assist in determining which descriptor the vessel fits. The subscription price to BucValue is well worth the price. Buyers have their own preference or tolerance for the amount of work they are willing to do after the sale. Some prefer to buy a "good deal" and do whatever restoration it takes to prepare the vessel to sail away. Others want a ready-to-go vessel and want only future maintenance to manage. My good sailing buddy Mark told me that a "quality," structurally sound vessel, ready for sale with little or no work required after the sale was his preference. He said just the monthly maintenance of the vessel was enough to manage. We were personally ready to take on a little more in the terms of restoration but definitely wanted to avoid having to deal with structural issues. In our case, I knew I could manage certain types of restoration work and get more boat for the money with the help of a good surveyor. Others are willing to buy a "poor to restorable" vessel if they can find one with "good bones." This means a vessel that has a structurally sound hull, keel, and engine that can be brought back to a useful sailing life. A surveyor of the highest order is needed to assist in these deals since structural damage is often out of sight and can be very hard to find in most vessels where access to the nether regions is very difficult due to the way the interior is constructed. A single-cracked stinger that is impossible to see could spell a nightmare ahead. That being said, there are cruising vessels out there that can be purchased for less than $50,000 and if brought back to life be worth much more.

Boat US has been our marine insurer for years, and they provide a free boat value service to their members who are either buying or selling their boat. I am not sure but I am guessing that they use all the surveys that come into their office as a guide for the boat values they publish since their values are consistently lower than BucValu.com. Brokers and surveyors have access to a website that list any given make of vessel that has sold within the last year. They know what the boats are actually selling for across any given world region. It is a service provided by

BoatWizard, part of the Yachtworld web site. Your broker may provide you with this information in some cases; it doesn't hurt to ask!

Yachtworld.com is not the only site to monitor. If you've narrowed the list to a top ten or fewer, Google the vessel make and "for sale" to locate a variety of sources including individuals selling a boat, auction sites, and craigslist.com. You do not need a broker to close the deal, but you will have to do all the work the brokers provide. For people with time this can save some money, as it can be a negotiation point. But you have to be on your toes and do your research to prevent worst-case scenarios from playing out. One such risk is buying from someone posing to own the boat who runs off with a big down payment. This occurred to an acquaintance we met in Florida.

Revisit boats on the web often to check for price reductions. This happened to us and can easily happen to most. When vessels first come on the market, the owner is determined to get what they fantasize as the vessels value. As time goes on, reality and reason prevail and price reductions occur. The survey adds another dose of reality to the seller. He can either accept or reject the surveyor's values of the vessel. In our case, the surveyor saved us thousands of dollars because we offered the market value stated on the survey and the seller accepted.

For us, selling and buying a vessel at the same time was not practical because of money and time. I do know individuals who were ready to buy, and they bought their next boat before the last one sold. Maintaining two vessels is not where we wanted to be. There were a couple of vessels we were watching that we really wanted to consider, but we stuck to our plan and let them slip away. We felt that if it did not work within our constraints, it meant the boats were not the right ones for us. If you are near the time that you are considering buying, then it might be helpful to have a frank discussion with your broker about the vessels on your top-ten list and start a search for an independent surveyor. You can buy a boat without a broker, but you need the surveyor to protect you from yourself!

Finally, be present at all the events involved in the purchase of the boat. Do not be absent for any of the things such as a sea trial, the surveyor's inspection, or the haul out at the yard. I know those who sent a representative in their place or hired a captain or let the broker do it. There is too much involved, and things can be overlooked when you are not present. It took both the Admiral and I to keep an eye on every detail and ask questions at every step to make sure our interests were a priority.

I will never forget a retired couple we met in Boot Key Harbor who had never sailed or owned a boat before, and they bought a forty-eight-foot 1948 steel ketch with no broker and no survey. They said the deal was just too good to pass by. I must have looked like a deer in headlights when they told me. They sailed the vessel all the way down the East Coast to Marathon, Florida. They said they had a few "incidents" along the way but made it to Boot Key Harbor!

13
HIRE AN "INDEPENDENT" SURVEYOR

Independent surveyors are the guys who do not owe anything to the local boat yards, brokers, or other marine services. They can cause a bit of consternation for the broker and the present owner. They will make sure you are buying a vessel that is structurally sound and not about to sink and help you get a fair price for the vessel. There might not be such a surveyor in the local area, but it pays to have one brought in from another area that is so well respected. It is recommended that you use a surveyor who is a member of the Society of American Surveyors (SAMS) http://www.marinesurvey.org/ or National Association of Marine Surveyors (NAMS) http://www.namsglobal.org/. You can check the websites to find a certified surveyor in your area. Once you have their name, you can search them online and usually find comments or reviews by other boaters who have used their services. Boat US has a list of surveyors online that they recommend. You can probably call your marine insurance company as well to find a surveyor they recommend for your area.

You are hiring the surveyor to complete a pre-purchase C&V (condition and valuation) survey that is required by marine insurance companies. The objective of the report is to describe the vessel and its condition at the time of survey and to set recommendations for correcting deficiencies found, which may have a negative effect on its value, structural integrity, and/or fitness for intended service. The conclusions of the survey are found in three sections of the report:

1. Observations that are lower-priority issues addressing any deficiency that could affect value, maintenance, or preservation of the vessel. Most of these items are not difficult to correct and do not pose a danger to the vessel of crew.

2.Recommendations that are high-priority issues addressing any deficiency that could affect the structure or safety of the vessel and crew.

3. Valuation is set forth an opinion as to the approximate fair-market value (FMV) and replacement cost new of the vessel at the time of survey. FMV was the only number that seemed to apply to us. I never really understood what the *replacement cost* number was for until now. I asked John Baird, an excellent Pacific Northwest surveyor who is currently helping us with our next vessel, to help me understand *replacement cost*. John said, "Replacement cost is for a new vessel (exact model or equal of similar quality and utility). I use it when establishing a FMV based on depreciation or remaining useful life model where a new replacement cost is required. Some insurance underwriters use it when setting premiums." I finally understand this number. It is a number that applies to new vessels. For used vessels, it is useful for those who may use their business to buy a recreational vessel and thereby depreciate the asset. For the wide majority of us, the number is of no use. Obviously the insurance companies can use the number for their formulas to determine premiums. Fair-market value is what the vessel will be insured for, so in the case of a total loss, that number would be the maximum the insured would receive minus any deductibles or other factors insurance companies use to decrease their liability.

In addition to the C&V survey, you should consider hiring a mechanical surveyor for the engine and for sailboats a certified rigger to survey the rigging. Often the C&V surveyor can point you to qualified and trustworthy contractors for this work. Always check out all the suggested surveyors online for reviews from other boaters who have used their services. If you cannot find any reviews or comments by others who have used their services, then be cautious.

If the engine is older or has lots of hours on it, having a mechanical survey prior to the C&V survey can determine if you want to continue on with the more expensive C&V survey. Published engine hours are *always* suspect. This includes the engine hours on the engine panel. A proper engine oil analysis can give you peace of mind. A mechanical surveyor can demonstrate to you the proper way to take an oil sample, which will come in handy. Later you can use this skill to keep an annual checkup on your engine. Note that a oil sample taken improperly will yield false results. There are plenty of Internet resources that discuss the uses of an oil sample analysis and the proper way to take one. An oil sample analysis (OSA) can help you determine the life left in an engine. These are relatively cheap and quick. An excellent article in the April 2015 edition of *Seaworthy Magazine* details the specifics of an OSA and explains the benefits. You can find it here: www.boatus.com/seaworthy/assets/pdf/seaworthy-april-2015.pdf. The article also gives an example of an OSA report at www.boatus.com/seaworthy/assets/pdf/oil-analysis-report.pdf, and further information can also be obtained from the Cashman fluid analysis at http://cashmanfluidsanalysis.com/. If there is any question about the transmission, you can also have an oil analysis for this important component as well.

If the standing rigging is twelve plus years old or in case the boat has been raced extensively or ocean cruised seven years or more, then a rigging inspection can spot immediate problems or just give you peace of mind knowing the whole rig is not going to come tumbling down. What looks like solid metal on the outside can be a hollow piece of metal corroding from the inside. A small ball-peen hammer will tell you the difference. I would not do this alone unless you have plenty of experience with rigging. A professional rigger can save you time and money. A friend went sailing on his 37' C&C on a light-wind day and he lost a shroud, causing his mast to break in half right above the first set of spreaders. He owned the boat since new; however, through the years, he never had a rigger inspect any part of the standing rigging.

When we bought our second boat, a Catalina 30, we learned that the yacht broker, the surveyor, and the boat yard all had their hand in the others' pocket. This is only natural in any business community. You do not want to make the same mistake we did by asking the yacht broker which surveyor is best to use! We were very naïve, but we chalked it all up to a positive learning experience preparing us for the moment when we approached buying our "most perfect" cruising boat.

Prior to visiting a vessel, we were interested in a marina on Liberty Bay in Poulsbo, Washington. I spent several evenings researching surveyors in the Puget Sound area and found Alain Vilage at www.ptmarinesurvey.com/quote.html. I knew I hit pay dirt when I found out all the area brokers disliked him and the buyers loved him. Traveling from Austin, Texas, to Puget Sound for us was not as crazy as it seemed, as the right vessel that fits your needs could lie anywhere. It is much better to go through a few more hoops to get the one you want than buy a boat that is geographically close but not exactly the one you preferred. Vilage saved us tens of thousands of dollars, literally. He provided the best survey and gave an honest value for the boat. He made suggestions that paid off tremendously in the restoration process and gave us a feeling that we finally understood the system and played the game well. He also agreed on our selection of boat yard to decommission the boat for the truck ride back to Texas. If *Mikey* likes it!

When we were having *Wand'rin Star* decommissioned in Port Townsend, Washington, for the trip back to Texas, there was a boat being hauled out in front of us. There were two thirty-something-year-old females with an awesome ocean racer sailboat, and Alain was surveying the vessel. I saw Alain near the travel lift and hollered out to him. I told him thank you for helping us buy the boat. He acknowledged and continued with the survey of the ocean racer. I asked one of the women if they were having the boat surveyed for a pending purchase, and she said no, adding that they are planning taking the boat across the Pacific Ocean to Hawaii and they needed a survey for the trip for their insurance company. Also they wanted to make sure the boat was ready to make such a trip.

I did not forget this encounter and decided that when we were ready to toss off the lines on a long-distance voyage, I would make sure to have a qualified professional to objectively survey the vessel. The Admiral and I have discussed several times the need to have an updated survey for

Wand'rin Star to get the insured value closer to our investment. I knew this would be important prior to departing on our cruise. As we neared our departure date we were having the boat hauled for a bottom job, I knew it was the right time to hire a surveyor. I called Mike Firestone, the most respected surveyor in the Coastal Bend, (361) 549-7767 firestone.mike@gmail.com. To prepare *Wand'rin Star* to go cruising, we spent thousand of dollars of upgrades and maintenance in the three years after the purchase. I did not expect to learn of new issues about our boat during the survey since I worked on the boat for so long and involved in the maintenance and upgrades. Firestone helped us immediately identify a problem with our rudder during a haul out and made suggestions in working with our insurance company. He spent several hours inspecting the hull throughout and assisted in directing the repairs to the rudder. The result was complete confidence in the repairs, and the out-of-water work completed in preparation for the cruise.

A couple of weeks passed by before he could return to complete the "in the water" portion of the survey. Firestone showed up at 0900 hours and did not stop till 1730 hours. I stayed by his side all the way through the survey. He found twenty-three items that needed attention. I could not believe it! His attention to detail was incredible. He pointed out things requiring attention or correcting throughout this portion of the survey. The repairs he found were small detailed items in nature and would be mostly my labor and just a boat buck to remedy, but they were much easier to correct prior to departing. Doing so made all the difference in having a successful two-year cruise with absolutely nothing breaking or coming apart along the way. Mike stated that we had done a very good job of preparing the boat for a cruise and said he would not hesitate to take the vessel in its current condition across an ocean. It is difficult to explain how I felt at that moment. To have my work validated by one of the most respected professionals on the Gulf Coast was thrilling. The next day, I began addressing the twenty-three items from his survey and simultaneously working on the two-page list I compiled to complete prior to departure. The minor $800 expense of his survey was worth thousands! Completing a predeparture survey was the best decision we made, by far.

The fact is, and you read it over and over again in the cruising and sailing magazines, you can never be 100 percent ready to cast off the lines. There is always something that needs attention. If you are going to go, then go and be ready to make unforeseen repairs on the way. After this survey, we felt mentally and physically prepared to depart. We spent the remaining time waiting for hurricane season to pass, completing all the remaining small projects. Keep in mind that there will always be small and not-so-small stuff to attend to. Paradise is not free.

Firestone is known as the surveyor you want to have if you are buying a boat and one that you do not want anywhere near your boat if you are selling one. I am sure there are many more such "independent" surveyors who do not owe anything to the yacht brokers or the boat yards for their business. But you have to do your research to find them. They are often in high demand and have a full schedule and do not need anything but word of mouth for advertising.

I caution against relying on self-surveys. Although this is a practical approach during the hunt process, you need a third party to protect you against yourself and provide legal recourse in the event the purchase goes south. Even if I were a knowledgeable boat builder, marine designer/architect, and three-time circumnavigator, I would not go through a substantial purchase without the safeguards a professional surveyor provides. Most marine insurance companies require a survey on pre-owned vessels. Almost every marina you will encounter will require a copy of your insurance at check in so it is very difficult to get by without a professional survey.

14
BUYING THE BOAT

You will now know it when you see it. Through this process, you will know as much, or more than, the present owner, broker, or surveyor by the time you step on the boat to make an offer. The things that you will not know are hidden to everyone except perhaps the present owner. These are your future boat projects.

For two reasons the buyer has the upper hand in the sales agreement. First and foremost, the buyer can walk away anytime during the process and have his deposit returned in full. Be sure to read the "Sales Agreement" (see appendix A) and understand every section of the contract. All the dates listed on the contract need to be updated if there is any delay in the several steps it takes to complete the process and close on the vessel. If you go through the whole process and neglect to close the deal, then you could be at risk of losing your deposit, which is customarily 10 percent of the purchase price. The deposit is then split fifty-fifty between the seller and the broker less any fees owed against the vessel such as unpaid surveyor cost.

Second, the buyer is fully prepared to assume the cost of ownership that includes the insurance, moorage, and maintenance of the vessel. All these costs have become liabilities for the seller. While these considerations are not mentioned in the process of the sale of the vessel, they are certainly encouraging the owner to complete the sale. The cost of owning a forty-foot vessel without loan payments can be in the $1,000 to $2,000 range monthly depending on the region where the vessel is moored. No one wants to bear this cost long if they are not enjoying the use of the vessel.

There were always two of us involved in the decision making because two heads are always better than one. Bob Stalbird, a good friend of mine from the San Antonio area, called me up and told me he would be in Austin to look at a boat he was considering to buy at Lake Travis. He asked me to go along since his wife would not be able to make the trip.

He obviously knew the value of having someone along to discuss the pros and cons. Bob and I each had our own set of questions for the seller so we covered a lot of ground. I could be very objective, since I did not have a stake in the vessel at all and I certainly wanted to look out for the welfare of my friend. While Bob was caught up in the fantasy of possibly owning and sailing the vessel, I was only concerned with what worked and did not work on the vessel. They did not end up buying the boat, but the experience demonstrated to me how valuable having a second opinion is to keep the fantasy from taking over your brain. So take a loved one or a close friend, who also knows something about boats, along when you step on the boat. Chuck Gustafson, in his book *How to Buy the Best Boat*, provides a pretty thorough evaluation checklist. But his Appendix H is missing two things on the checklist: modern electronics and an objective friend.

If the vessel is being sold through a brokerage, it can be to your advantage to have your own broker as a representative in the deal. This does not cost you anything since the seller pays all commissions. The broker will prepare a written offer called a purchase and sale agreement, which must be submitted to the listing broker along with your 10 percent deposit. That deposit will be held in the listing broker's dedicated escrow account.

A word of caution: If a broker doesn't have a dedicated escrow account for this purpose, this should be a red flag. You might want to find another broker. You can find if your broker is certified by CPYD (Certified Professional Yacht Broker) at <u>www.cpyb.net</u>.

The first step in the process is to make a personal inspection of the vessel arranged by your broker. Take a knowledgeable person to help thoroughly go through the vessel from bow to stern inside and out (*two heads are better than one*). You will need a couple of flashlights so that you can see every nook and cranny as you inspect the lockers, cabinets, and storage areas. Do not be shy. Remove cushions and any other gear so that you can gain access to every area. Take pictures of everything as you go through your inspection including any documents like invoices and owners' papers that are in the chart table or stored elsewhere. Careful inspection of the bilge and keel bolts, hull components like stringers, engine, bulkheads, and the chainplates first makes sense due to the fact that if any of these areas are compromised, then you may not want to continue the process. Take pictures of the tag on the engine with the model and serial number, the engine hour meter, and any suspect areas like rusty motor mounts. Often a camera will see things your eyes cannot. The camera seems to pick up differences in slight color changes better than our eyes. When we viewed the digital photos at home, we could easily zoom in on our laptop and see where repairs were done in bilge or hull areas that we could not see before. Small cracks were easier to differentiate between flaking paint or actual cracks in the fiberglass. Photograph the electrical panel and all navigational equipment and electronics including the model numbers. Take your time and write notes as you go along. This is also the time to find out exactly what equipment will convey with the purchase. You may not be able to determine an accurate and complete list but now is the time to start that conversation and be sure you have it all in writing before you sign a purchase agreement. Your pictures will come in handy to help recall everything you inspected later on. If you need to inspect the vessel a second time later, do not hesitate to ask, but if you do a through job the first time, the second look can be brief just to confirm what you saw the first time.

There is a disclaimer that is on every listing on yachtworld.com or other sites similar to this:

Disclaimer

The Company offers the details of this vessel in good faith but cannot guarantee or warrant the accuracy of this information nor warrant the condition of the vessel. A buyer should instruct his agents, or his surveyors, to investigate such details as the buyer desires validated. This vessel is offered subject to prior sale, price change, or withdrawal without notice.

If later, after you sign the purchase agreement, after the survey, and/or you close the purchase, things are not what you thought, then the only way to find the person responsible is to look in a mirror. The above disclaimer makes sure of that. A good surveyor will make every effort to save you from yourself, but there are limits to everything!

Next research the history of the vessel you are considering. It is much easier with all the Internet resources, but it takes time commitment. The Admiral is much better at this than I am. She is very detail oriented, and I tend to see the big picture, which is a good combination. Here is a list of ways to get at the boat's history.

You can start with a list of questions for the owner. Our recent experience hunting for our Pacific Northwest sailboat evolved into a list of questions that we e-mailed to the broker and asked him to forward to the owner to answer:

1. What is the age of the standing rigging including chain plates?

2. Has the vessel ever been involved in a collision with any other object or run aground?

3. Has there ever been any repair work to the hull, keel/keel bolts, rudder, mast step, or shaft/strut/prop?

4. Is there a maintenance log available?

5. Are there invoices for any repairs available?

6. How many past owners?

7. Has the vessel ever been in charter, if so what years and with what company?

If the owner is not forthcoming with information, then there is certainly a reason why. The owner and broker may not be conducive to answering the questions unless you have made an offer on the vessel. I would in that case just make it understood that it is expected to have the answers before proceeding with a survey. As a buyer, you have the right to ask any question related to the safety and value of the vessel.

The brokers will assist in encouraging the seller to be forthcoming, but in the end, the seller may only disclose information that will encourage the sale. This is why the buyer must be thorough in researching the vessel's history. In our search we have experienced owners who were 100 percent cooperative: those who avoided anything that might be construed as negative and those who refused to answer any questions at all. We made it clear that even if a vessel had some repairs, we just wanted to make sure that a competent shipwright did the repair work and we wanted to see the invoice. If the repairs are done correctly, they are better than brand-new production work. We would call the company that performed the work discuss the repair and then forward the information to our surveyor.

Find all the previous owners' names. It is always good to know all the previous owners. It is usually just a few search clicks to find a previous owner's contact information. Call, e-mail, or write to them and ask them the same questions as above about the vessel. On one occasion, we had an address but no phone or e-mail contact. I wrote the person a letter, and he called us. He was very nice and answered all of our questions and invited us to contact him anytime we had any other questions. Most will love talking about their time with the vessel and provide you valuable insights. A few might not want to talk about it at all. I tried to contact the seller of our cruising vessel after the sale to ask about some unlabeled switches. We did not know what they were for. He never returned our calls or e-mails. I reached out again through our broker, hoping he could get the information for us. He forwarded the questions but didn't receive a response. At this point, I knew he was done with the vessel and did not want to be bothered.

Depending on the situation, more owners can either be a great thing or not so great. Every time a vessel sells, the new owner usually completes a lot of initial maintenance and installs upgrades and/or restoration work. We were the fifth owner of our vessel. I did not have the information of three owners until after the purchase. But later the second owner actually contacted us and provided all the information we needed to get up to speed on the history of the vessel, the upgrades, and maintenance records. Social-media sites like Facebook can be helpful in identifying and contacting previous owners. If you have a Coast Guard documentation number or a boat name, you can search the Coast Guard documentation website for ownership information. You can find Coast Guard documentation number search page at www.st.nmfs.noaa.gov/st1/CoastGuard/VesselByID.html. You can do the same on most state agencies boat registration websites. You normally need the owner's name, address, and the boat's state registration and/or the hull number, which is usually found engraved on the upper topside of the stern usually under the toe or rub rail.

Obtain work orders/invoices: Each owner customizes the vessel according to his needs and vision. In many cases, they pay a boat yard to do the work and so you can get the records from the boat yard if they are not available from the seller. You definitely want to have these records. Boat yards are more than willing to provide them to you, as they know you might provide them some business if you buy the vessel. The person we bought the vessel from had extensive restoration work and upgrades done by two different yards, so we were able to contact them before, during, and after the sale for records. One of the last projects we completed before sailing away was to replace the aging fuel and water tanks. Here is where I learned. When boat yards install new electrical or electronics, they cut the old connections and install them new. Since we had access during the tank replacement to the nether regions of the vessel, I removed several pounds of wire that ran to nowhere. One respected sailor on the docks told me that eliminating hundreds of feet of useless corroding wiring was one of the best things I could have done for the vessel.

Search Vessel Owners Association: You can search the owners' association (such as www.endeavoursowners.com) to learn many details about the vessel. The primary purpose of most owners' association is to provide help in maintaining, repairing, and upgrading their vessels. You can usually search a vessel by boat name, hull number, or owners' name. Gaining access to the threads where the owner posted comments will provide details about the vessel.

Personal contact with others who know the vessel's history: You can gain some history of the vessel by talking to other boaters on the docks where the vessel is moored. Just walking the dock on a weekend can lead to finding neighbors who know the boat and can provide insight. But always take what they say, either positive or negative, with a grain of salt. Strangers owe you nothing and may have other intentions that are not in your interest. Also if the previous owner belonged to a boat club or association, you can call members and learn details that can lead you toward a complete history.

You may now be ready to make an offer. Your broker will submit the offer and negotiate with the listing broker on your behalf. The seller can reject it, accept it, or make a counteroffer. Once the buyer and seller agree on the price and terms of the sale, the buyer will post a 10 percent deposit into an escrow account. The buyer's broker will assist in setting up a sea trial. Your broker might also refer you to a professional yacht surveyor, but I advise you to choose your own surveyor who will inspect the boat for you. I strongly recommend that the surveyor be on board during the sea trial. In our case we sailed the boat across Puget Sound to the nearest boat yard that could handle a haul out for a boat our size. The surveyor conducted the survey during the sea trial, was present for the haul out, and accompanied us on the trip back giving him plenty of time to evaluate the boat in both under sail and motoring conditions. If the survey or sea trial uncovers a defect in the boat, several options are open to the buyer. The buyer can do the following:

1. Reject the vessel outright and get a full refund of the money deposited in escrow.

2. Ask to have the defect fixed before accepting the boat. If you exercise this option, then the buyer should select the boat yard and oversee the repairs to protect from substandard work.

3. Renegotiate the price down and fix the boat after the sale. This option is best for those who will move the boat to a new region. It would be difficult to get the boat back to the repair yard hundreds of miles away for warranty work. Having the work done near your home port seems a better decision to me in most cases.

Many brokers now encourage the seller to offer a *repair allowance* rather than a renegotiated sales price to cover the cost of repairs. The repair allowance is money back to the buyer at closing thereby protecting the brokers 10% commission on the original offer. This is a clever way to insure the broker gets paid based commission on the original offer. This can cost the buyer as well since he has to pay sales tax on the final selling price. Broker Kent Little offered these insights from the brokers perspective:

You mentioned commissions on the boats being based on the original selling price and after survey the seller fixes stuff or gives cash back at closing to cover it and the broker leaves it at the original price and gets commission on that. Somewhat true but it's a case by case basis. I've also had 100K boats that had 50K wrong with them and they sold for 50K after and they were the work of a 300K boat to get it to work even at the $50K. In that case the brokers are worth what they are paid on the higher end. 90% of the time we adjust the commission to accommodate the new selling price.

We recently bought our next vessel in California and shipped the vessel to Washington state. After working with the DMV in Washington State we had the broker provide a revised final statement with *Total Price Paid* on the bottom line of the statement and along with the engine survey which showed a $5,000 repair estimate we paid our taxes on $63,000 rather than the $68,000 selling price shown on the original buyers final statement. Every state is different and so calling the department responsible for registering boats in your state can save you hundreds of dollars or more by making sure you present them with the amount you actually paid for the vessel on the bottom line of the "Bill of Sale" or "Buyers Final Statement".

Of course, the buyer pays for the survey and the cost of hauling the boat out of the water for inspection and any related boat yard fees. If an agreement can't be reached, then the buyer loses this cost. But that is the cost of insuring you do not get into a deal that could be much more costly in the long run. In some agreements, there is no provision for price negotiation. As the buyer, you should ensure that a negotiation provision is in the offer agreement *before* your broker submits it to the listing broker.

After the survey and once you and the seller agree on the final price, the buyer's broker will continue to assist you by offering financing options, determining taxes, and making sure the yacht has clear title with no outstanding liens or encumbrances. This ensures that the ownership will pass smoothly to you during the closing. Because a buyer's broker offers so many valuable services, you can see why it makes sense to have a dedicated representative looking out for your interests throughout the process. And again, what's not to like about free?

If you are buying from an individual and not through a broker, then understand you will have to do all the work when it comes to protecting your money and investment. I have both bought and sold a vessel without a broker being involved, and I can testify that selling without a broker is the most difficult since you have to be available to show the boat to lots of people who have no intention of buying. When buying a boat, you have to make sure the seller actually owns and has a clear title to the vessel. You can do this by getting a copy of the title from the owner and or getting the hull and registration number. If the vessel is US Coast Guard documented, obtaining the Coast Guard documentation number and checking with those agencies to see who is listed as the owner is important. Also it is smart to find out if the owner owes any money on the vessel. If he has a loan on it, find contact information of the bank and call to determine if there are any other liens and the balance of the loan. It would be smart to close the deal at your bank or lender's place of business to ensure that you get a clear title with no other outstanding liens or encumbrances from any source, such as a boat yard and so on.

Usually individual sellers do not require a 10 percent deposit. If your survey and other concerns are fully addressed, then you may have bought yourself a boat. Individuals sell their boats because they do not want to pay the 10 percent brokerage fee. So that means they would probably turn down any request from a broker representing your interest unless perhaps the broker is willing to negotiate a lower fee with the seller. When we sold our first two vessels without a broker, we met at the bank of the person purchasing the boat and the bank officer efficiently managed the transaction.

Your dreamboat rarely evolves into the perfect boat. Perfect boats do not exist no matter how much money you have; there are always compromises. Although you have done plenty of homework by now, there will be unforeseen events that change the way you view the "perfect boat." Instead it will be the "most perfect" boat. Armed with the following information, you are ready to close the deal:

1. The regional market highs and lows for the vessel you are considering from www.yachtworld.com
2. The published BucValu
3. An accurate list of the equipment that conveys with the vessel. Do not trust the inventory listed on Yachtworld.com, often these list are not accurate. Have the owner or broker sign off on agreed inventory that conveys with the sale. It is up to the buyer to make sure the equipment is in good working order.
4. Previous boat yard work orders/invoices
5. Any information gained by boat history research
6. The C&V survey

Making the deal is not so much different from buying big-ticket items like a car or house. Chapter 15 in Chuck Gustafson's *How to Buy the Best Boat* is probably one of the more important. His recommendations on negotiating are spot on. (Personally, I think we have a bit of the same blood in our body.) When I first found *Wand'rin Star* for sale on Yachtworld.com, the asking price was $160,000. The owner spent nearly $20,000 on the boat installing all new standing rigging, new upgraded battery system, and new electronics. They only owned the boat for a little over a year before unforeseen circumstances forced them to sell the vessel. A year later, when I started to become interested in the boat, the price dropped to $125,000. Only after the excellent survey (conducted by Alain Vilage) valued the vessel at $105,000, we adjusted our offer to the surveyed value. I called my broker Kent Little and told him our revised offer. He said, "That is too low. He won't take it." I told Kent that was the best I could do, and if it did not work out, then I was going to hop on a plane to see a Tayana 42 that came up for sale in Florida. Less than an hour later, Kent called up and said, "You just bought a boat."

If there are repairs that need to be completed before the sale is final, be sure you have the voice on who and where the work is done. Do not let others fix your soon-to-be boat. You choose the boat yard and oversee the repairs to your satisfaction. Determine a limit to what you are prepared to spend for the negotiated deal and stick to it, unless they throw in extras that sweeten the deal. The money you do not spend on buying the boat will come in handy outfitting it to your liking. If your offer is not taken, and you feel that you have given a reasonable offer, then it was not the boat that was meant for you. There are other options that will serve you just fine on your top-ten list. My experience buying boats reminds me of the first new car I purchased in 1972. I shopped two different Toyota dealers. One offered $25 less for the same vehicle in a different color. When I told the dealer of the more expensive car that if he matched the deal, I would buy his. He got insulted and yelled, "All this for $25?" I told him, "Yep, it's our money" and I thanked him for working with us. We walked out and bought the cheaper one inside an hour. The Toyota salesman of the vehicle we purchased was courteous and happy he made the sell. The point is to have an option at hand when you make the offer. If one does not work out, the other one will and it will be the "most perfect" boat for sure.

When we bought our Endeavour 42 in Puget Sound, both the brokers split the $10,500 fee the seller paid. My broker in Kemah, Texas, certainly worked with us for two years and was instrumental in helping us find our vessel. But, when the sale came, he only had some telephone consulting and co-brokerage work to do with the broker in Poulsbo, Washington. The Poulsbo broker spent three days with us showing the boat, being there for the survey, and doing follow-up after the sale. We signed all the paperwork in his office.

Buying the "most perfect" sailboat is like writing the perfect song using just eighty-eight black-and-white keys on a piano. Some will love the song, but to others it will sound like fingernails on a chalkboard. To others your "most perfect" boat may be

1. Too big or too small
2. Too heavy or too light
3. Too slow (*One very good inland sailor told me I should buy a fast boat so we could outrun storms. On a lake you might be able to make it back to your marina before the storm hits, but if you are sailing in coastal or the open ocean, there is no vessel fast enough*) or too fast
4. Too much maintenance or too complicated
5. Too much plastic, or too much wood
6. Too unsafe or any other things that concern particular sailors

It is not about their dream. It is about your dreams. When you get to the point that you are ready to step aboard and get on with it, then allow your dream to reemerge from the fog of all you have learned about boats and fall in love with the spirit of the vessel and get her ready to sail away.

Our sailing friend, Andy, bought a Taswell 42 sailboat as his very first boat. I was stunned to learn he never owned a boat before and he bought this blue-water yacht. He approached the process "differently." He was young and had years to go before retiring from his job. He bought the boat to live on and learn to sail. In the meantime, he restored the vessel and he sails often with others crewing on one of the fastest racers on Corpus Christi Bay and cruising with friends. By the time he is able to retire, he will be more than ready to sail away.

15
PREPARING YOUR VESSEL TO SAIL AWAY

With a thorough survey detailing issues that need immediate attention, the cosmetic fixes can wait. You are now ready to begin the final stages of preparing your vessel; however, keep in mind the most important things are often out of sight. There is a old saying that goes "Cruising is fixing broken stuff in exotic ports." As you go through the process of checking all systems to make sure they are ready to go, be sure to start a maintenance log with detailed information including part numbers and all actions taken. There are a lot of electronic forms available that can help you in this process, including apps for your smart devices.

1. Leaks: Charlie Teat said to me in his Texas drawl, "Steve, make sure the water stays on the outside." Stopping any and all leaks should be high priority. Even brand-new boats come with leaks, especially if they have been trucked to a location. Boats were made to travel by the complete support that water provides to the hull. When a boat is loaded onto a trailer with the keel supporting all its weight and bouncing down bumpy roads, the leaks can develop from the entire hull flexing or wherever there are screws, hatches, portlights, and other metal hardware attached to the fiberglass. There are numerous solutions and materials for stopping leaks. You need to be really proficient at this. I take great pride in having a dry bilge. This way, if I ever see water in the bilge, I can track it down immediately to find the source. If you keep a wet bilge, it can be difficult to know where the water may be coming from. My Admiral is like a Labrador when it comes to leaks. She can spot the tiniest trickle and remind me with steady encouragement to take care of it.

2. Standing and running rigging, including chain plates: Do not skimp here. Use the highest quality gear, and make it user-friendly. Remember: a professional rigger will save you time and money.

3. Auxiliary engine: It's amazing how often your destination coincidently is in the same direction as where the wind is blowing. When cruising on

a sailboat, you will do more motoring than anyone led you to believe. Be sure your auxiliary engine is in excellent condition and have plenty of spare filters, belts, hoses, and impellers plus enough oil for two to three oil changes. Engines that are infrequently used go through v-belts more than those are not used a lot. Why? Because the sheaves on the v-belt pulleys will rust if the engine is not used often. Then when the engine runs, the rust wears down the v-belts as it polishes off the rust from the sheave. The sheave can rust over again if the engine is not run for weeks, and then the rust will eat at the belts again when the engine is started up. The same thing happens on cars. But since most of us use our cars daily, the pulleys and sheaves stay shiny and smooth so v-belts last a long time.

4. Ground tackle: There are plenty of books on proper anchoring gear; learn about it, and make sure you have adequate ground tackle to make it through a tropical storm. Most cruisers carry three anchors for different bottom types, that is, mud, grass, or rock. Practice anchoring in high winds, and see how your gear holds. Setting any type of anchor is an art that takes plenty of patience and lots of practice. Having your anchor drag is bad enough when you are on board. Just think of the feeling you might have if your onshore and you see your vessel is dragging off into unknown danger. We have our own learning curve regarding dragging anchor and have witnessed several other vessels dragging directly toward us in a crowded anchorage. We fortunately were on board and quickly resolved the situation twice, and one other occasion when we were not onboard, we were able to dingy back to the vessel and avert a disaster. These turned out to be very important experiences for us since no harm was done and the learning paid off for us on our two-year cruise around the Gulf of Mexico to the Florida Keys and back. We never drug anchor on our cruise due to proper safeguards. Active Captain developed an app called DragQueen anchor alarm and works great for your smart devices. On one other occasion, when we were in the British Virgin Islands on a charter vessel at a small reef island, a couple of sailors told us our vessel was dragging. We jumped in their dingy and soon found it was not our vessel but another

one just like it. It drifted over a mile away and was nearing a huge cliff with big rocky shores. We managed to get on board and return the 46' Jeaneau to the young couples who were blissfully enjoying a great day snorkeling around the reef.

All types of windless anchor are subjected to the constant saltwater spray coming over the bow. Service your windless frequently and always give them a freshwater spraying whenever possible.

5. Sails: If the sails are nearing the need for replacement, then do it. You will have the old ones for spares. The first sail to buy new is a storm jib or storm trysail. Rig a spare halyard just for that reason. You may never use it, but if the time comes and you need one, you *really need* one!

6. Water tanks: Take care of your tanks. Keep them clean, and keep any corrosion at bay on the fittings. We use a portable water filter that we attach to the shore-side water hose every time we fill our tanks to keep sediment out of the tanks. When we replaced the water tanks in *Wand'rin Star*, I had to cut the largest tank in half to get it out of the companionway. I was surprised to find a lot of sand in the tank! We also installed an onboard heavy-duty water filter that filters the water as it leaves the tanks. This keeps all your plumbing hoses and faucets clean and insures clean water throughout the system. Chlorine bleach can be used to disinfect stale water tanks, but it is corrosive for aluminum and stainless steel tanks. Hydrogen peroxide has been used as a substitute, and there are some commercial products available. As a note of caution, that any US city water usually has some level of chlorine in it. If you are not using your onboard freshwater system regularly, then drain the tanks. When you resume, run plenty of freshwater through all the plumbing systems to get the system ready to use again.

7. Fuel tanks: A Dual Racor fuel filter with a pressure gauge will make changing fuel filters easy and even possible while the engine is running. I know it may seem counterintuitive, but use a four-micron filter in the dual system. This will keep even the smallest debris out of the engine and since you can change the filters easily anytime, it is a no-brainer.

Just make a habit to pay attention to the pressure gauge on the filter system.

8. Rudder and steering gear: We replaced the stuffing in the gland around the rudder post as a result of a very slow leak of water. Our Edson steering system required replacing some of the conduit and a steering cable. Be sure you can lubricate the whole system. There are upgrades you can install for that purpose in the event your system does not have a way to keep the steering system lubricated.

9. Through hulls and bottom paint: Always inspect every through hull at every haul out and lubricate them. If you spot any corrosion or other issue surrounding the reliability of any through hull, then replace them. Bottom paints are a regional thing. It has to do with the temperature of the water and the type of marine growth that you will be dealing with. To find out what type and brand of bottom paint works best in their waters, ask seasoned boaters where you plan to sail.

10. The bilge: Clean and dry are my strongest recommendations. This is one area that reveals the most about the owner. If the bilge is wet, full of water, dirty, or smelly, then the owner clearly does not practice the most basic principles of vessel maintenance. If you have a bilge that has constant standing water, it is difficult to determine where the water is coming from. Dirty bilges risk the pumps that serve to keep them dry. A dry bilge smells much better and it affords the owner to track down any new sources of leaks whether it is from rain water, sea water, condensation, or from the onboard plumbing. If you have a standard packing gland on the shaft, then upgrading to a dripless is well worth the cost. Many bilge pump systems leave a residual inch or two of water in the bilge. Properly installed bilge pumps, hoses, and bilge pump switches will drain all the water. These systems are usually more costly than the standard systems installed in many vessels. It is worth the upgrade.

11. Safety gear: Go beyond what the coast guard requires you to carry. Read up on SOLAS-approved safety gear and head in that direction.

They once held a flare-and-smoke demonstration at our marina and all the cheaper gear was difficult to see from a distance. Only the SOLAS-approved equipment performed in a way that had the best chance of actually being seen by someone far away. Save old flares etc. that have expired dates. They will last a few years beyond the expiration and they will serve as backup in the case you need them.

12. Electronics: Save adding the latest electronics to the final preparation stage. Some of the electronics on our boat were only two years old when we bought the vessel. But two years later, when we added AIS and updated our charts we realized our equipment was aging compared to the latest standards. Our backup portable was a Garmin chart plotter that was no longer supported by Garmin, so we had to turn to third party software to update those charts. The iPad and other smart devices have definitely changed the game. The major electronics companies are rushing to stop the bleeding by making their products compatible with onboard wireless Wi-Fi systems and tablets. What used to require a $3,000 investment for GPS can now be bought for the cost of a second-generation iPad and a $20–50 app with your iPhone acting as a backup! Few under the age of forty-five in 2017 are interested in any of the expensive electronics still being sold to the older generations.

13. Active Captain: The online cruising guide https://activecaptain.com/ is integrated into several brands of chart plotters software programs. If you have not used Active Captain before, then it is time to register for free online. It is quickly replacing any paper or book type cruising guides because it is updated in real-time by thousands of cruisers. This is a worldwide resource, and the features of the guide are growing exponentially.

14. Using your laptop or PC-based tablet as a second or even primary chartplotter: With Freeware like SeaClear II (www.sping.com/seaclear/) or Open CPN (http://opencpn.org/ocpn/), you can connect a USB GPS antenna and even interface with the other electronics onboard thorough NEMA 2000. We use SeaClear II for route planning and as a chart plotter backup. Many users prefer Open CPN, but I think the

preference has more to do with which program you decide to learn first. The great thing about these resources is that you can download updated charts free from NOAA for either program. So updated charts and the chart plotting software are free! If you want to integrate into the other electronic systems onboard, get a bit of wiring and a USB GPS antenna, which cost about $25. Both have user groups on Yahoo! so you can join the group and get free support. Every boating community likely includes people with knowledge on the topics, so ask around, and I bet someone can help you get started. If you are interested in Seaclear II, then you can find a "How to" primer on our blog at http://svwandrinstar.blogspot.com/2015/11/seaclear-ii-how-to-use-this-pc-based.html.

Early on in the hunt for our boat, we met with Captain Bill, who accompanied us on the sea trial for our second vessel. He had years of experience doing boat deliveries, sea trials, and general boat captain work on all types of recreational vessels all over the Gulf of Mexico and beyond. We had our coastal cruising certifications and wanted to begin to explore opportunities to cruise on the Gulf of Mexico. So we asked for his advice on the best way to begin the cruising experience once we found our "perfect" vessel. He said,

A lot of people buy their cruising boat, make it around Florida and then immediately take off to the Bahamas. They start having things break or fail and it is costly to have things shipped and repaired far away from the United States. My advice is to cruise the Eastern coast of the United States the first year to make sure all systems are working properly and get to know your boat. That way it is easy to get repairs and parts in the United States where everything is still readily available and relatively inexpensive. Afterward, if you are still inspired, then take off through the islands.

The strong practicality of his advice rang true to us.

One last piece of advice from Charlie Teats: "You can't have to many fenders"!

16
SELLING YOUR DREAM BOAT

For whatever reason your life takes a turn and you put your dreamboat up for sale. This happened to us as I was writing this book so I feel it is important to include this side of the experience. In our case, our Seattle family called and informed us they were pregnant and would have their first child in August. Our daughter asked us to come to Seattle for six months to assist. We were so excited that we decided to sail our boat back across the Gulf of Mexico and put her in a slip in Corpus Christi. We drove to Seattle to be grandparents. Long story short, six months turned into three years, and we decided that we loved the Pacific Northwest and wanted to begin our next sailing life in the Puget Sound region.

We had a major decision to consider: Should we truck our vessel back to Puget Sound or sell her and buy a vessel around the Seattle area? Believe me, I fantasized about sailing around through the Panama Canal, but that was not in the cards. It would be a three-month or longer journey, and I would need to recruit an able crew and prepare the boat for the trip. The cost of such a journey would be equal to the cost of trucking the boat across the United States. As we discussed our goals for a Puget Sound boat, our needs have changed. No longer would we need such a large vessel, something in the thirty-six-foot to thirty-seven-foot range would be best for our future needs. We would no longer be living on the boat full time and since we are not getting younger, a smaller, easier-to-handle vessel would be smart. We decided to sell *Wand'rin Star* and buy a vessel in our new waters.

I flew back to Texas and recruited my friend, Jeffery Konop, as crew to sail to Kemah, Texas. We put the boat in the Little Yacht Brokerage. That's right. I took the boat back to the broker who sold it to me as he knew the boat well. He now owned his own brokerage, the largest one on the Texas Gulf Coast. I moved the boat from Corpus Christi to Kemah because large cruising vessels languish for a year or several waiting for a buyer to come along in the smaller coastal communities. If you want your vessel to be seen by lots of buyers, then you need to take it to the big brokerage markets. Most of the vessels that sell in the Corpus Christi area are in the 25'–35' range or smaller. The large majority of people looking for a boat in this area are interested in weekend boats, or small coastal cruisers to cruise the local area for two to three day weekends.

This was the first time for us to *sell* a boat through a broker. I thought I had a pretty good handle on it, but it is different on the seller's side of the contract. I knew a few things about selling a boat such as the following:

1. The owners' personal gear needs to be completely removed so that the prospective buyer can inspect all the cabinets and lockers inside and out. For me this took six days to complete. We had a lot of personal gear, and it required renting a storage space nearby and about six truckloads to transport. The only things that are left in the interior or exterior of a vessel are those things that will be sold along with the vessel.

2. The interior needs to be completely detailed and clean. I completed all this work in about four full days. I thoroughly cleaned every square inch in all the nooks and crannies including the engine room. Smell is also very important, and you have to eliminate any boat odors. A dehumidifier and plenty of ventilation go a long way, and your cleaning should have solved any lingering mildew issues. You can pay to have all this done, but I had the time and needed to save this expense.

3. The exterior clean and buffed to a perfect shine. Our vessel was in a brokerage dock next to gleaming, shining vessels. I knew that ours had to look as good if it was going to be noticed. A less inviting vessel in this neighborhood would just get a walk-by. I hired a local detailer for this. I paid $1,400 for the service and definitely got my monies worth. I always kept our vessel clean and waxed. For a 42' boat, this was a yearly job that took me six full days to do, and I mean twelve-hour days. A professional job looked way better. In fact *Wand'rin Star* never looked so good since we owned the boat. I was amazed that they were able to

get a 1987 hull-and-deck to look brand new. I did not have the time to commit to all the exterior work and I could never have achieved the same results as these professionals.

There was more for us to learn as we went through the process of selling through a broker. Selling our dreamboat was not exactly one of the best days in our lives. It was a hard decision, one where we looked into the future and had to come to terms with realistic goals for the next several years. We were also managing the sale through a broker long distance. We were in Seattle and the brokerage in Kemah, Texas. Even though I spent a month in Kemah preparing the vessel for sale and working closely with the brokerage so that their staff would have a working knowledge of the vessel and all the work we had put into the boat, being physically so far away was a huge disadvantage. Due to our experience, I strongly encourage those who are selling their boat to be available on standby during the whole process. No one knows your vessel the way you do, and working through several middlemen toward a successful sale has several challenges that being available in person would solve.

The survey during the sale process turned up four issues: the mast step, some delamination on the deck around the mast, black smoke from the engine above 2,000 RPM, and a nonworking windlass. The next step after the survey, if the buyer wants to proceed, is to get quotes from local contractors to correct the issues. This is where it gets sticky if you are not physically there to oversee this process. While the buyer should be the person who chooses the contractors he was also far away on the East Coast. So he entrusted the broker to do that for him. This is an immediate red flag since the brokers and the contractors all feed from the same basket. The quotes for resolving the issues were all over the place and exceeded $15,000. I began to call contractors and talk to them directly to slow this mad rush to my bank account. I worked with a mechanic and resolved the engine issue for $1,300. I shut down the $1,200 repair quote for the windless by explaining to the broker the issue could be fixed with a singe allen wrench and about thirty minutes of time. The expensive quote on the mast step was also shut down, as I knew this was a nonissue. Any corrosion on the step could easily be wiped off with a few strokes of a wire brush. They originally told me the mast step and the end of the mast were compromised. The mast step would have to be replaced and the end of the mast may have to be cut a few inches, resulting in having a new mast step fabricated to be taller to account for the amount cut off from the end of the mast. So I intervened with the contractor, and since they had to remove the mast to correct the twelve inches of delamination on the deck, it was resolved since there was no corrosion on the foot of the mast or mast step. In order to stop the bleeding on the quote for the delamination repair, I drew a line in the sand. I offered $8,000 to be put in a escrow account from the sale for repairs. Once I drew the line, somehow all the feeding frenzy stopped.

This took many e-mails, calls, and text over the course of a month to navigate. If I were present I could have easily addressed the concerns without all the stressful e-mails and text. I would have been able to get the work done by quality contractors for less than $5,000. That of course would have required me doing some of the work and spending another six weeks in Kemah. The seller has more obligations than the buyer. The seller has signed an agreement to sell the vessel and has some obligation to satisfy the issues found in the surveys. The seller can sell the vessel "as is" and not agree to a reduction in the initially agreed selling price, but then they are most likely risking the sale of the vessel. Additionally, the seller has the burden of the monthly cost of moorage, insurance, and regular maintenance that have become liabilities weighing heavily on his side of the sale.

The important thing to take away from our experience is to understand the relationship between the buyer, seller, and broker. When you sell directly to a buyer, there is direct communication. Brokers offer a valuable service in managing the sale, and they earn their commission, but their objective is to close the deal. Brokers often modify the communication between the seller and the buyer to achieve the deal.

They have a balancing act to keep both parties engaged and to complete the sales contract. What the seller hears from the buyer is modified through the broker's voice and vice versa. In the background are a host of other players who line up for a piece of the deal whether they are the detailers, the surveyors, mechanics, riggers, or shipwrights. They all live and work in close proximity and, as I said, feed from the same bowl. If the owner is not physically present, then it seems that the players have a license to maximize their earnings from the deal.

I think that a good way to detail the process of selling your dreamboat is through the use of the Sale Agreement that you and the buyer are required to sign once an offer has been made. The example in Appendix A is from a broker here in the Seattle area where we are actively in the process of buying our next vessel. Each brokerage has their own twist on this contract so be sure to read the contract carefully before signing and ask questions. Make sure you understand fully your responsibilities and liabilities under the Sales Agreement. This is where having a trusted broker who will guide you through the process and act as a advisor will serve you well. Just know that there are several players who will profit from the sale of the boat including a possible co-broker. When a buyer uses a co-broker, then you have two modified voices between the seller and buyer. In some cases the brokerage does not allow for co-brokers so, in that case, the *listing broker* supposedly acts fifty–fifty for the buyer and seller. This is very hard to do in any case; the bottom line is no one makes money if the boat does not sell and brokers invest considerable time and resources to close the sale. The broker acts 100 percent for the sale. Look over the document below, and in the following pages, I will comment on each section as it applies to the buyer and seller where appropriate. Often the seller and buyer will be presented a one-page document that summarizes the several page sales agreements in Appendix A.

I am attempting to offer some details of the sales contract. Note that I am not a certified broker or attorney so the following comments are those that I think are important based on our buying and selling experiences. Protect your interest, and be sure you have a complete understanding of the sales-agreement contract the broker puts in front of you by asking questions. Just as in buying, it is much better to have two heads review the document. The Admiral and I went through the details together. So have your mate, friend, or a close relative go through the process with you.

Refer to the sales agreement in Appendix A:

Top Section: Names the buyer and seller. If you are buying, include all those who you want on the title of the vessel. In our case, we had both of us on the title in case anything happened where one of us were not able to be present. Be exact when going over the listing of the vessel, as often brokerages do not include a complete inventory of items that should be included in the sale. Often pictures on the Internet show items that are not included so go over every detail to make sure the broker, buyer, and seller agree on what equipment is conveyed in the sale and what is not included. Sellers sometimes do not list equipment like dingy and outboard motor. They use these items as things to include in later negotiations to make the sale.

1. Price and deposit: In most cases, the prospective buyer has inspected the vessel before making an offer. Experienced buyers know the market and understand that the process on Yachtword.com are usually marked somewhere from 5 to 10 percent above actual market value. Other resources such as BucValu.com and marine insurance companies like BoatUS can offer assistance in determining a vessels fair-market value in any given market in the United States and in the world. This is the price the buyer has offered and the seller has accepted. The buyer writes a check, usually for 10 percent of the offer to be placed in escrow with the brokerage. This is earnest money that implies that the buyer is committed to the purchase. It also serves as a security deposit in the event that the buyer backs out of the deal to pay for any charges against the vessel during the buying process like survey and haul out cost. If the buyer goes all the way through the process and reneges on the

purchase, then the buyer can lose the deposit. The seller and the broker would split the deposit minus any charges due.

2. Survey: The surveys and haul out are the responsibility of the buyer but are often scheduled by the listing broker who is responsible for assisting in getting these events completed in a timely manner. The buyer chooses the surveyor and the haul-out yard. A survey can easily find issues that the seller was completely unaware of. Prudent buyers may have more than one type of survey. For older vessels, a mechanical and a rigging survey can reveal issues not determined in the more common prepurchase condition and value (C&V) survey required by most insurers. If there are known repairs or upgrades that the buyer plans to complete, then they will oversee the contractors who will do the work. The buyer should list in the contract the types of surveys they want to have completed. It is common for sailboats to list three surveys: C&V survey, mechanical (engine) survey, and rigging survey. All parties should pay attention to the dates listed for the surveys. In some areas, especially during prime season, surveyors are very busy and it may be several weeks before the preferred surveyor can be scheduled. If for any reason the date of the scheduled survey exceeds the date on the sales agreement, the agreement should be updated with the new date and initialed by all parties.

3. Acceptance of the yacht: Acceptance by the buyer will be determined by the surveys, and the buyer will either

1. Accept as is.
2. If issues are revealed, then reject and end the contract.
3. Renegotiate a price reduction based on the survey fair market value and/or quotes for repairs. Some brokerages call this a "repair allowance." The repair allowance is paid back to the buyer at closing. Brokerages use this strategy to maintain the original offer amount so they can maximize their commission from the sale. For the seller, this means they will pay 10 percent of the original offer to the broker. For the buyer, this means they will pay sales tax on the original offer amount. This strategy only benefits the broker. Only a price reduction benefits both the seller and buyer. As a seller I would simply renegotiate

the sales price period. As a buyer, If you find yourself in this situation, then insist that the bottom line of the *Bill of Sale* or the *Buyers Final Statement* shows *Total Amount Buyer Paid* and keep copies of surveys to show to the department in your state that registers boats.

The quotes for repairs should be completely overseen by the buyer. This means choosing the companies to complete a quote. In some cases, the seller reduces the amount of the negotiated price based on the quotes for repairs, and then the boat is sold as is. In other cases, the sales contract closing date is extended to allow for repairs to be completed. The buyer is responsible for overseeing the repairs. As a seller I would not want to be held accountable for faulty work so I would want to be involved in the repair process and approve the contractors given that after repairs the buyer may not complete the purchase.

4. Termination of agreement: If the buyer rejects the vessel, he or she will receive a full refund of the deposit given that he or she paid out of pocket for any and all survey-related cost if the dates on the sales agreement is met. If the date for acceptance is exceeded, then the buyer will risk losing the entire deposit. It is in the interest of the buyer and seller to pay particular attention to all sections where dates are listed. If for any reason the dates for any section seem difficult by either party to meet, then be sure to have them amended. If extra time is required to get the necessary quotes for repairs, then ask to have the dates amended and agreed upon by all parties. It may take two to three weeks before the deposit is returned to the buyer since the brokerage has to ensure that any charges against the vessel have been paid in full.

5. Closing: The happiest day for a boater is when he or she buys a boat or when he or she sells one's boat. This may be true for the buyer in a brokerage deal, but for the seller, he or she will depart with 10 percent of the selling price as brokerage fees. The seller is, however, relieved to be free of his or her monthly cost of ownership. The buyer certainly needs to be prepared for the cost of sales taxes and state registration or Coast Guard documentation. Some states also have property or excise taxes. The buyer also needs to make sure he or she has an active

insurance policy on the date of closing! So while the seller is parting with 10 percent of the purchase price to the broker, the buyer can easily be parting with an additional 10 percent for taxes, insurance, registration, and surveys. Then the buyer needs a place to moor the vessel. The buyer is very happy anyway because he or she is going sailing in his or her new boat! Some brokerages have in-house staff who manage the title and fund transfer. Other smaller brokerages will use a title company, and the buyer will pay those closing expenses.

6. Additional provisions: First state the conditions for the buyers financing of the vessel. As the buyer, I would always claim that the sale is dependent on "satisfactory financing" even if you plan to pay cash. This prevents a seller or broker from trying to force the sale since it is assumed there is a lender who has to approve the financing. The other additional provisions for the buyer to write in are the additional surveys like mechanical and rigging or any other concerns that the buyer may have regarding the sale of the vessel.

7. The seller's other rights, obligations, and miscellaneous provisions: The benefit here is that the broker often provides a title and registration service or they work through a title company, in which case the buyer will have to also pay the title company fees. This ensures the buyer gets a clean title free from any liens, bills, or other encumbrances against the vessel. It also provides a convenient service to the buyer to have the vessel appropriately registered in their name. The broker or title company also handles all money transactions and thereby protects their commission and their interest as a broker. The seller gets a check for the final agreed amount minus the commission to the broker. The buyer gets the vessel and all the equipment listed on the inventory at the date of closing. For the seller, the date listed in this section means that his or her obligation to sell the vessel expires after the date listed, so pay attention to dates.

8. The buyer's obligations to satisfactorily complete the financial transaction: The buyer writes a check or transfers funds for the agreed amount plus title, registration fees, and taxes minus his or her deposit.

Usually the buyer pays the fees for the surveys and haul-out expenses out of pocket; however, in some cases the fees can be paid from the deposit and the amount paid to the broker adjusted equally. This could occur in cases where the buyer is not present for the surveys. This would be a huge mistake in most cases on the part of the buyer in my opinion.

9. The seller's interim responsibilities. In some cases, the seller is present during the sea trial and on the trip to and from the yard for haul out. The reason is that marine insurance companies only insure the vessel when the owner is in command of the vessel. There are a few brokerages that have certified captains who are bonded, and so they carry their own insurance. In these cases, the owner is not required to be onboard. If the owner is onboard, this is the buyer's chance to have all questions about the vessel answered, so come with a list of questions and take notes on everything. This is another reason why having a friend or your wife along helps with this part. After the sale is over, the owner may refuse to answer any more questions. When we sold *Wand'rin Star*, the buyer called about a week later and I gladly spent an hour or so answering questions and making sure he had a good start. I invited him to call anytime he had a question. An interesting note here is the person I bought the boat from was a retired Coast Guard captain, and the person who bought the boat from us was an active Coast Guard captain.

10. Default by the seller: If the seller defaults for reasons in his or her control, then it can get expensive as the seller may be required to pay for the charges incurred by the buyer such as surveys and related cost. In addition, they are required to pay the broker their commission. If the default is not the seller's fault, he or she may still have to pay the buyer's expenses but is forgiven the commission to the broker. The buyer is refunded his or her deposit.

11. Default by the buyer: Basically if the terms of sale have been honored by the seller and the buyer defaults, then the broker and seller split the deposit fifty-fifty less any charges against the vessel. This

means that if the buyer gets cold feet, he or she better throw in the towel early if the person wants his or deposit back. If he or she waits beyond the date of closing, the brokers can be aggressive about keeping the deposit. This is important so I will restate: if the surveys reveals issues with the boat, the buyer can walk away right then, or if the seller refuses to lower the price to have the boat repaired, then it is time to walk away. You can always terminate the contract and negotiate a new sales agreement after the dust settles. Remember that the broker is invested in completing the sale. He or she is skilled at assisting the seller to make realistic decisions to close the deal. In our case, this occurred when we were selling our boat. We had a backup plan of taking our boat off the market and trucking the vessel to Puget Sound and were fully prepared to do so. Both the buyer and seller need a backup plan. Neither should feel that there is no other outcome. We managed to work on a daily basis with the broker and the contractors who were hired by the brokerage to complete the repairs within the limits that we determined.

12–15. Arbitration of disputes: These sections basically protect the brokers. It pits the seller against the buyer if the contract hits the fan, so to speak. The broker is saying they are at no fault, and either the seller or buyer or both will be responsible for any attorney fees or court. So you can see that if they have to put all this in a sales contract, then it is prudent for the buyer and seller to completely understand the contract and the process it defines. I have seen several of these contracts to date, and each one is a little bit different, so be sure to go over the details carefully with the broker until you understand your obligations and your liabilities.

Afterthoughts

The intent of this chapter is to provide the reader a holistic perspective in the process of buying and selling. Initially it was going to be a *How to Buy Your Most Perfect Boat*. Serendipity occurred as I was nearing the completion of the book and we sold our "most perfect boat" and started searching for the next one. My daughter Lia, the editor, advised me to include the selling portion. After putting our beloved vessel on the market with a broker for the first time and living through the selling side of the brokerage experience, it became crystal clear that to best understand the process, you need all the parties' perspectives, interest, and motivations to fully grasp the dynamics involved in buying or selling a cruising boat. I feel the most important aspect of the process is to be present throughout the experience.

Additionally, our hunt for our Pacific Northwest sailboat to cruise the protected waters of Puget Sound led us on a journey lasting eight months and stretched from Anacortes, Washington, to San Francisco Bay. After making offers on five different vessels that failed our test, we finally found our next "most perfect boat"—a 1998 Catalina 36 on San Francisco Bay. Mark Minor of Rubicon Yachts was the listing broker and gave us first-class service. NAMS certified surveyor Kent Parker of Parker Marine Consultants and Mechanical Surveyor Chuck Thomas of Chuck's Marine met all of our expectations and put our interest first. Each of these six experiences contributed in its own way to the completion of this book.

Our favorite quote is "The difference between adventure and ordeal is attitude," by Bob Bitchen. We always thought of this quote in the terms of the cruisers' world. For cruisers if things go awry, so what? You're in paradise! The quote certainly applies to the process of buying and selling boats as well.

What better place than this to insert this little story:

Way back when we first started sailing at Canyon Lake, Texas, we drove into the parking lot of the marina just in time to see a thirty-plus foot sailboat arriving by truck. We noticed some of our fellow Hill Country Yacht Club members gathering to watch the boat have the mast stepped and backed down the ramp to the water. The young family was thrilled. The couple were young professionals with three boys so had lots of good times ahead for them. Then I heard the story on how they purchased the boat. The father found the boat listed for sale online. He liked what he saw and called the broker in Louisiana. With the broker's help, he arranged for a surveyor from long distance. He hired the surveyor over phone and received the survey by e-mail. The survey was satisfactory so he bought the boat and with the broker's help had the boat moved to a yard and arranged for a transporter to truck the boat to Canyon Lake, Texas. He said they just did not have the time to make a trip to Louisiana and so never made a trip to Louisiana, meet the broker, surveyor, or any one else involved in the deal. We were standing a few feet from them when they saw the boat for the first time as it arrived in the parking lot. The next weekend they were out sailing on this gem of a lake with their boys having a great time. They loved their boat.

Fair Seas

APPENDIX A

YACHT PURCHASE AND SALE AGREEMENT

This is an Agreement (the "Agreement") made by and between
_____, of _____, a citizen of
_____ (the "BUYER"), and _____, (the "SELLER"),
owner of the _____, described in the attached inventory which is
made a part hereof, and named _____, (the "YACHT"). The BUYER
and the SELLER recognize **Mighty Fine YACHTS** (the "SELLING BROKER") AND
_____, (the "LISTING BROKER") as the brokers handling the sale
of the YACHT, and herein referred to collectively as the 'BROKERS."

1.**PRICE AND DEPOSIT:** The "selling price" shall be
_____, **(U.S_____)** for which
the BUYER agrees to buy and the SELLER agrees to sell the YACHT, subject to the terms
and conditions set forth in this Agreement. The sum of
_____, **(U.S_____)** of the selling price
shall be paid as a deposit (the "deposit") upon execution of this agreement. The deposit
shall be paid to and held in trust by the SELLING BROKER pending resolution of this sale.
The balance of the SELLING PRICE shall be paid in cashiers, certified or collected funds at
the closing.

2.**SURVEY:** The BUYER may have the YACHT surveyed at his expense, on or before
_____**20___**, to verify the condition of the yacht and the accuracy of the
attached inventory.

a.The SELLER agrees that BUYER or his agents may examine the YACHT and inventory in
a nondestructive manner. The SELLER may stipulate at which boatyard he is willing to
have the YACHT hauled for survey. The SELLER agrees that delivery to and from the
boatyard for survey, which he hereby authorizes, is to be at the SELLER's sole risk and
expense.

b.The BUYER agrees that the surveyor(s) shall be employed by the BUYER, and that the
BROKERS are not responsible for any errors, omissions or other inaccuracies that may
appear on the survey of the YACHT, even though the BROKERS may have suggested the
name of the surveyor, or at the BUYER's request, may have hired the surveyor on behalf
of the BUYER.

3.**ACCEPTANCE OF THE YACHT:** The BUYER shall notify the SELLING BROKER in writing of
his acceptance of the YACHT and inventory, his rejection of the YACHT, or his intention
to request repairs or a price adjustment for same, no later than five o'clock p.m. local
time on _____,20___. If said notice has not been timely received, the

BUYER shall be deemed to have **rejected** the YACHT and inventory in its present condition, subject to the terms, if any, of paragraph #6. IT IS THE BUYER'S RESPONSIBILITY TO OBTAIN ANY ASSURANCES HE REQUIRES REGARDING THE AVAILABILITY OF SATISFACTORY FINANCING AND INSURANCE PRIOR TO THE ABOVE MENTIONED DATE.

4.**TERMINATION OF AGREEMENT:** If the BUYER gives notice of his intention to reject the YACHT under the terms of this Agreement, such notice shall constitute termination of the BUYER's obligation to purchase and the SELLER's obligation to sell, and the BUYER and the SELLER both authorize the SELLING BROKER to return the deposit to the BUYER, after deducting any fees and charges incurred against the YACHT by the BUYER, or by the BROKERS on behalf of the BUYER, including the cost of the survey and related expenses.

5.**CLOSING**: The "closing" on this sale shall take place on or before _____, **20___**. local time, at the office of **PACIFIC MARITIME TITLE CO. SEATTLE WA.**

the closing on the sale shall be deemed completed when:

a.All documents necessary to transfer good and absolute title to the YACHT have been received by the BUYER, or by the SELLING BROKER on behalf of the BUYER; and

b.The balance of the SELLING PRICE is paid in certified or collected funds to the SELLER, or to the SELLING BROKER for transmittal to the SELLER.

6.**ADDITIONAL PROVISIONS:** (if none, write "NONE" in the space provided)

FINANCING: Yes__No__   Waived   _____   Date   _____   *DEMO   SAIL:*
Yes__No__Waive_____Date_____

Other: _____**Date**
Waived_____,20____.

Other: _____Date Waived
_____,20____.

OTHER RIGHTS, OBLIGATIONS AND MISCELLANEOUS PROVISION

7.The SELLER warrants and/or agrees as follows:

a.That he has full power and legal authority to execute and perform this Agreement, that he has good and marketable title to the YACHT, and that he will obtain permission from any authority to sell the YACHT, if necessary.

b.That the YACHT will be sold free and clear of any mortgages, liens, bills, encumbrances, or claims whatsoever. If any such obligations remain outstanding at the closing, the SELLER authorizes the SELLING BROKER to deduct the funds necessary to satisfy such obligations from the proceeds of the sale.

c.To deliver the YACHT and its inventory as accepted in paragraph #3, on or before _____, 20___ at _____.

d.To pay any and all duties, taxes, fees, or other charges assessed against the YACHT by any governmental authority prior to the closing, to hold harmless and indemnify the BUYER and BROKERS against any claims or actions for such fees, and to provide validation of such payments at the closing, upon written request by the BUYER, ten days prior to the closing.

e.To hold harmless and defend the BUYER and BROKERS against any and all claims incurred prior to closing that may impair or adversely affect the BUYER's receipt, use and possession of the YACHT including good and absolute title thereto; and to assume all costs incident to defending BUYERS and BROKERS against such claims, including their reasonable attorney's fees.

f.To pay the BROKERS the commission as soon as the sale is consummated, and authorizes the BROKERS to deduct the commission from payments received directly or indirectly from the BUYER. Such commission shall be calculated upon the above stated selling price without regard to subsequent adjustments as a result of survey or otherwise. Should the sale not be consummated for any reason, and the SELLER transfers any interest in the YACHT to the BUYER, directly or indirectly, within two years of the closing date of the Agreement (except a charter of one month or less); then the SELLER agrees to pay the BROKERS an amount equal to the commission which would have applied to the sale for which this Agreement is now created.

g.Must accept or reject this offer on or before _____.

8.The BUYER warrants and/or agrees as follows:

a.That he has full power and legal authority to execute and perform this Agreement, and to obtain the permission of any authority to buy the YACHT, if required.

b.To deliver the following at closing:

1.Certified or collected funds payable to the SELLER, or for the SELLER's account, in an amount equal to the balance of the selling price as set forth in Paragraph #1.

2.Certified or collected funds payable to the BROKERS, in an amount equal to any charges incurred against the YACHT by the BROKERS on behalf of the BUYER, including costs related to any survey of the YACHT.

3.Any and all documents, including authorization, required to complete this purchase.

c.To pay all sales and/or use taxes, now or hereafter, imposed as a result of this sale, to indemnify the SELLER and BROKERS against any obligations to pay such taxes, and to furnish proof of such payments upon request by the BROKERS.

d.The BUYER will have the right of possession of the YACHT only upon completion of the closing.

9.**INTERIM RESPONSIBILITIES:** SELLER agrees to be present at sea-trial or a representative of SELLER will be on board. YACHT will be delivered to sale), shall obligate the SELLER to pay all costs and charges incurred in connection with any survey undertaken on behalf of the BUYER, and to pay the BROKERS the full brokerage commission which would have otherwise been due pursuant to paragraph #7. SELLER's obligation is without prejudice to any other rights the BUYER might also have as a result of SELLER's default. However, if the sale cannot be completed by the closing date, due to substantial damage to the YACHT not caused by the SELLER's negligence, the SELLING Broker is authorized to deduct from the deposit, any fees or charges incurred against the YACHT by the BUYER, including the cost of the survey and related expenses, and return the balance to the BUYER.

11.**DEFAULT BY BUYER:** The BUYER and SELLER agree that the amount of damages sustainable in the event of a default by the BUYER are not capable of ascertainment. Therefore, in the event that the BUYER, after accepting the YACHT under the terms of this Agreement, fails to fulfill any or all the obligations set forth in paragraph #8, the deposit shall be retained by the SELLER as liquidated and agreed damages and the BUYER and SELLER shall be relieved of all obligations under the Agreement. This sum shall be divided equally (50%/50%) between the SELLER and the BROKERS after all expenses incurred against the YACHT by the BUYER have been paid. The BROKERS' share shall not exceed the amount the BROKERS would have received had the sale been completed.

12.**ARBITRATION OF DISPUTES:** Any dispute, controversy or claim relating to this Agreement, including but not limited to the interpretation thereof, or its breach or existence, which cannot be resolved amicably by the BUYER, SELLER or BROKER shall be referred to arbitration, which shall be the sole and exclusive forum for resolution and settlement of any dispute, controversy or claim between the parties. The arbitration shall be conducted in accordance with the Rules of the American Arbitration Association then in force and shall be held in the city and state of the SELLING BROKER's office unless the BUYER and SELLER mutually agree upon another place. Any award of the arbitral authority shall be final and binding upon the BUYER, SELLER or BROKER with respect to all disputes, claims or controversies encompassed therein and the BUYER, SELLER or BROKER shall comply with said award without delay. The arbitral court have jurisdiction over the party against which the award has been rendered or where assets of the party against which the award has been rendered can be located. The BUYER and SELLER further understand and agree that arbitration shall be the sole and exclusive forum for resolving any dispute, controversy or claim relating to this Agreement and that neither party shall resort to any court except to compel arbitration, refer questions of law or to confirm, vacate or modify any such award.

13. Should the LISTING BROKER or the SELLING BROKER become party to any litigation involving this Agreement and found not to be at fault, it is agreed that the BROKER(S) shall be reimbursed for costs and attorney's fees by the party(s) found to be at fault.

14. This Agreement shall:

a.   be construed and interpreted in accordance with, and the arbitral authority shall apply the substantive and procedural law of the State of the SELLING BROKER's principal office;

b.   constitute the entire Agreement between the BUYER and SELLER, and supersedes all prior discussions, agreements and understandings of any nature between them, and may not be changed or added to except by agreement in writing and signed by the parties to be bound;

c.   be binding upon and shall inure to the benefit of and be enforceable by the successors in interest of the BUYER and SELLER, including but not limited to heirs, executors, administrators or assigns;

d.   survive the closing of the transaction, and shall not be merged in or otherwise be affected by the execution, tender, delivery or acceptance of the Bill of Sale or any other documents executed or delivered at the closing.

15. THE BUYER EXPRESSLY AGREES THAT NO WARRANTIES OR REPRESENTATIONS, EXPRESS OR IMPLIED HAVE BEEN OR WILL BE MADE DIRECTLY OR INDIRECTLY, BY THE SELLER OR BROKERS, CONCERNING THE CONDITION OR USE OF THE YACHT. THE BUYER FURTHER EXPRESSLY AGREES THAT HE HAS NOT RELIED UPON ANY ORAL REPRESENTATION BY THE SELLER OR THE BROKERS AS TO THE CONDITION OR CAPABILITY OF THE YACHT OR ITS INVENTORY. THE BUYER ALSO RECOGNIZES AND ACKNOWLEDGES THAT YACHTS AND THEIR INVENTORY MAY HAVE BOTH APPARENT AND/OR HIDDEN DEFECTS AND BUYER ACCEPTS RESPONSIBILITY FOR DETERMINING THE CONDITION OF THE YACHT, ITS INVENTORY AND THE EXISTENCE OF ANY DEFECTS. and returned from survey yard by SELLER or representative of SELLER. It is specifically agreed and understood that BROKER does not assume and is not delegated care, custody or control of YACHT by reason of this agreement. The SELLER agrees to deliver the YACHT and inventory to the BUYER at Seattle WA on or before _____.

The SELLER shall bear all risk of loss or damage to the YACHT, or to any person or property on said YACHT until closing. Any damages to the YACHT subsequent to acceptance as set forth in paragraph #3, and prior to completion of closing, shall be repaired by the SELLER at his expense, subject to approval of the BUYER, who has the right to request a reasonable price adjustment or to cancel the sale if substantial damages cannot be repaired to his satisfaction.

10. **DEFAULT BY SELLER:** SELLER's failure to deliver the YACHT to the BUYER or otherwise to perform the terms of this Agreement, due to any reason (including loss of or substantial damage to the YACHT caused by the SELLER's negligence which prevents completion of this

***** **SIGNATURES** *****

Purchaser(s):   X _____   _____   Date: _____

Seller(s): _____   _____   Date: _____

Broker: _____   Date: _____

BIBLIOGRAPHY

Bitchin, Bob. *Vintage Attitude-The Perfect Boat.* Cruising Outpost: http://cruisingoutpost.com/2015/04/vintage-attitude-perfect-boat/ April, 2015.

Byrne, Rhonda. *The Secret.* New York: Atria Books, 2006.

Gustafson, Chuck. *How to Buy the Best Sailboat.* New York: Hearst Marine Books, 1991.

Marshall, Roger. *Complete Guide to Choosing a Cruising Sailboat.* Camden, ME: International Marine, 1999.

Mazon, Allison. *Oil Sample Analysis. Seaworthy, BoatUS Marine Insurance* 33, No.2 (2015): 10–11.

Nestor, Gregg. *Twenty Affordable Sailboats to Take You Anywhere.* Arcata, CA: Paradise Cay Publications, 2007.

Perry, Robert. *Sailboat Design I Sailing Designs: 79 Contemporary Sailboat Designs Analyzed* (Volume I). Port Washington, WI: Port Publications, 1977.

Perry, Robert. *Sailing Designs: 109 Contemporary Sailboats Analyzed* (Volume II). Port Washington, WI: Port Publications, 1980.

Petrillo, Renee D. *A Sail of Two Idiots. 100 Hard Lessons from a Non Sailor (and Her Husband) Who Quit the Rat Race and Sailed to a New Life in the Caribbean.* Chicago: International Marine/McGraw Hill, 2012. Print

Robinson, Ed. *Leap of Faith: Quit Your Job and Live on a Boat.* N.p.: OutskirtsPress, 2013. Print.

Seifert, Bill and Spurr, Daniel. *Offshore Sailing: 200 Essential Passagemaking Tips*. New York: International Marine /McGraw-Hill, 2002.

Siegal, Jeff. "Active Captain-The Interactive Cruising Guidebook." Web. 2015. Retrieved from https://activecaptain.com/

Slocum, Joshua. *Sailing Alone around the World*. New York: W. W. Norton & Company, 1984.

Vigor, John. *The Seaworthy Offshore Sailboat: A Guide to Essential Features, Gear, and Handling*. Camden, ME: International Marine, 1999.

ABOUT THE AUTHOR

Steve and daughter Lia Sailing the San Juans

Author Steve Steakley developed his interest in sailing in his early twenties crewing aboard the Chris Craft 31 SV *BarTom*. He participated in club races for three years at the Fort Worth Boat Club on Eagle Mountain Lake. In three years of racing, the crew of *BarTom* placed only one time during a Frost Bite Regatta when the weather was so bad and the other three starters turned back. It was their only chance to place so they stayed the course through the finish. Later, after his kids were grown and out the door, he bought his first sailboat a Catalina 250 in 2001 and joined the Hill Country Yacht Club on Canyon Lake, Texas, where he became a volunteer Boating Certification Instructor for the Texas Parks and Wildlife Department. He and his wife participated in club races, placing several times in the *Cruising Class*. In the summer of 2002, they crewed with HCYC friends on a chartered bare boat in the British Virgin Islands. They took their first American Sailing Association Keelboat Certification in Corpus Christi with Captain John Lillard. In summer of 2004 they purchased *Hey You* a 1986 Catalina 30 and moved their sailing to Lake Travis, Texas. Here he learned to restore boat systems and stop leaks. In 2005, they earned their 103 Coastal Cruising, 104 Bareboat Cruising, and Navigation ASA Certification in

Kemah, Texas, on Galveston Bay with Captain Ralph Brannem. In 2006, they chartered a Fontain Pajot 46 Catamaran in Belize with friends from HCYC.

In the summer of 2007, Steve secured a position as a captain for Just For Fun, skippering fifty passenger party barges, eighty-foot houseboats, and working with the SeaTow operations. In August 2007, they bareboat chartered a Tayana 42 for a week of sailing in the San Juan Islands. In November 2007 he earned his USCG Merchant Marine 50-ton Masters with sailing and towing endorsements for inland waters. In July 2008, they bought their beloved 1986 Endeavour 42 *Wand'rin Star* in Poulsbo, Washington and sailed her to Port Townsend for decommissioning for the trip back to Texas. Steve crewed aboard the Erickson 36 *Apotheker* during two Harvest Moon Regattas, a overnight race down the Texas coast from Galveston to Port Aransas. The crew celebrated a third place finish in 2010. In November 2011, they tossed off the lines in Corpus Christi and Coastal Cruised the GICW and Coastal waters of the Gulf of Mexico for two years to Marathon, Florida, and back again on a seven-day voyage across the Gulf of Mexico from St. Petersburg, FL. to Corpus Christi, Texas. Steve and Lynn paused their cruise to go to Seattle, Washington, to be grandparents for the newest addition to the family. Steve works at the Center For Wooden Boats for as a Volunteer Sailing Instructor in their *Sail Now!* program. You can follow Steve at his blog: svwandrinstar.blogspot.com/

About the Editor

Lia Steakley Dicker received her master's at the Stanford University School of Journalism. She has written for *Northwest Construction Magazine*, *Seattle Metropolitan*, *Wired,* and *Business 2.0* magazines. She authored the book *Dream it, List it, Do it.* Most recently, she works as the social-media producer and wrote the media blog for the Stanford University School of Medical Research. She lives in Seattle.

VINTAGE ATTITUDE—THE PERFECT BOAT
April 4, 2015

What is the perfect cruising boat? I don't know how many times I've been asked that question. The answer is, there's no such animal. Unequivocally, period. Now there are people out there who really like what they have, but, if you'll notice, they are always in a state of flux. Did you ever meet a boater who wasn't working on something to make his boat better? Of course not. It's a way of life.

I remember about 15 years ago, when I had a boat I was pretty much happy with. I didn't have any projects going. No improvements in mind. I was just sailing it and enjoying it. Her name was *Predator*, and she was a Formosa 51. Right about now "performance cruisers" are chomping at the bit. "A Formosa 51! It won't get out of its own way!" they shout. "It won't sail tighter than 50° on the weather!" they scream.

Yeah. So? What's your point? Maybe I didn't want to go fast. Back in those days I had plenty of time to get there, so I was happy. But one afternoon I was sailing into port, feeling pretty spiffy, as we turned on the wind and dropped the sails smartly. Billy Jack dropped the headsail, Gina dropped the Mizzen and I dropped the main, like clockwork. We were looking good! We had spent the previous week laying on some varnish, and the stainless gleamed.

As it turned out, we were looking a little too good. Unbeknownst to us, there was a gentleman having a late lunch at the Lighthouse restaurant, with his broker. He'd flown in from Alaska looking for a boat, and hadn't found one. Until he saw *Predator*.

The broker met us on the dock. "Hey, ya want to sell that boat?" he asked.

Well, you know how it is, you never say no to a question like that. If you're happy with your boat at the time, you just jack the price up. Everything's got a price, right?

"Yeah, sure." I said, and I named an exorbitant price. Twice what I'd paid for the boat just a year earlier.

"Mind if I show my client?" he asked.

A half hour later I was standing scratching my head, wondering what had taken place. I had sold my boat. It was Sunday, and we would haul for survey on Monday. If all went well, I would have a week to vacate.

Uh. What happened? I was happy. For the first time in untold years I had a boat with no projects.

But maybe a boat that was a little faster? How about one that would sail into the wind at 27°? That would be nice. Maybe something a little newer? More fiberglass and less teak to varnish. That'd be good. Right?

Two weeks later I was moving onto a brand new 42 foot performance cruiser. It had less than an "hour's worth" of teak, could be single handed by any dolt, even me! Below decks it was pristine and simple. Kewl! I named her *Assailant*, and took off on our maiden voyage.

It wasn't three months later I was shopping for another Taiwan Turkey. Sure *Assailant* was fast. Yeah, she was easy to handle. There was almost no maintenance, and she almost maintained herself. The perfect boat, right?

No way, dude! She had about as much personality and character as a Tupperware container. It wasn't until late one night, I was in my dinghy after an evening doing 12 ounce curls at the Harbor Lounge. I was looking for my boat and I realized, I didn't recognize it. My boat looked just like everyone else's! Waugh!

As most folks know, I did find a project. The Lost Soul. My friends thought I'd slipped a gear or two. To sell a new, "perfect" boat, and buy one that is closer to sinking than not. It was just crazy. But the first moment I walked onto her teak decks, complete with missing caulking and bent stanchions, I was home.

And then I realized the truth of the situation. There is no perfect boat. There is just the boat that's right for you. How do you know it? What do you look for? Well, as soon as you step aboard it feels like home. Logic doesn't enter into it, though logical we all strive to be when looking.

As illogical as it all sounds, part of the joy I get from cruising includes those days when I stand, screaming "I hate boats!"

So the next time you see a neighbor, shirt all greasy, blood dripping from a wounded paw that got hooked on an old cotter key (yeah, it happens to us all), pity him not. Know that, in reality, this is the fun part. Remember this. The more hard fought the battle, the more heartfelt the victory. You gotta slay a dragon or two to kiss the princess.

I'll see ya. I'm goin'a go work on my boat!

(Reprinted with permission by Bob Bitchin.)

Sailing the Dream on Puget Sound with the Admiral.
Follow our Blog at: svwandrinstar.blogspot.com/

For their review and contributions many thanks to:

Mark Babcock

Jim Clower

Kristin Pederson

Final Review and edits by Vicky, CreateSpace Editor. The entire team at Create Space was extremely professional, helpful and considerate whenever I called upon them as a first time author and publisher.

50479319R00073

Made in the USA
Middletown, DE
31 October 2017

FINDING GOLIATH AND FRED
A Novel of Saratoga, 1777

By
Sandra E. McBride

First published by Dog Ear Publishing
4010 W. 86th Street, Ste H
Indianapolis, IN 46268
www.dogearpublishing.net

dog ear
PUBLISHING

ISBN: 978-159858-878-1

Printed in the United States of America

Dedication

To Allison, Tom, Jacob, Shannon, Grady, Meghan, Sam, Ryan, Martin, Erika, Emily, Spencer, Maggie, Matthew, Nathan, Seth and Benjamin. You are always my inspiration. Leave strong handprints and gentle footprints, for you are tomorrow's history.

Chapter 1:

Monday August 18, 1777

It was the night of the Full Red Moon when Liam Ratch came slinking through the woods and stole Goliath and Fred. I was in the woodshed gathering an armload of wood for the morning's cook fire when I heard the rattle of falling gate bars and the shuffling of feet. I set the wood back on the pile. Quiet as an Indian, keeping to the deep shadows, I crouched low and crept around the barn and up to the rail fence. There in the dim moonlight was Mr. Ratch, a tall slithery man, adjusting the big, heavy yoke on the oxen's necks.

"Git along!" Mr. Ratch hissed at Goliath, tugging at the yoke.

I stood up straight and climbed onto the bottom rail of the fence so I'd look real tall. "Hey!" I hollered in the bossiest voice I could muster. "Leave those oxen be! Josiah is coming with his musket. Josiah! Over here! It's Mr. Ratch!"

Mr. Ratch stopped in his tracks and looked over at me, a look that sucked the courage right out of me. Then he laughed.

"Who you tryin' to fool with, girl?" He walked over close to where I stood. "Your brother ain't here. He's down at the meeting-house with all the other rebel riffraff plotting to get themselves killed when Gentleman Johnny Burgoyne and his army comes marchin' through here."

Mr. Ratch was close enough that I could smell the rum on his breath and see the whitish cast of his blind eye. He was awful scary-looking, with his ragged beard and toothless grin, standing there in the moonlight with nothing between us but a split-rail fence. My heart was pounding so hard I was sure he could hear it.

"You'd best get out of here before Josiah does come back," I said, trying to sound braver than I felt. I stepped back down from the rail. How I wished Ma would come out looking for me, or Josiah would come up the path. "I won't even tell Josiah you tried to steal our oxen if you just go away."

Mr. Ratch laughed. "The British army will pay me in gold for these oxen," he said, his voice high-pitched and rat-squeaky. "Ain't no half-pint girl stoppin' me from takin' them, neither."

Moonlight glinted on the blade of the knife he pulled from his belt. I took two steps backwards. Mr. Ratch vaulted over the fence. I turned on my heel, hiked up my skirt and skedaddled for the cabin as fast as I could go.

"Ma!" I shrieked. "Help me!"

Mr. Ratch was right on my heels, splashing through puddles. When I was but a dozen steps from the house, he grabbed my shoulder and spun me around. Suddenly, candle glow from the opening door lit up his twisted face and glinted off the knife he held up over my head. A loud explosion split the night air. Liam Ratch shoved me to the ground, turned and ran off into the shadows.

Ma helped me to my feet, Pa's smoking musket cradled in her right arm. "Who was that?" she demanded.

"Mr. Ratch," I stammered, out of breath. "He's taking Goliath and Fred."

Ma reloaded the musket and ran to the stock pen. I hurried along after her, but we were too late. The pen was empty. Liam Ratch and our ox team had disappeared into the sultry August night.

Chapter 2-

Monday, August 18, 1777

"Are you sure it was Mr. Ratch?" Josiah demanded.

"As sure as I am that I'm Annie Blair," I said. "He was as close to me as I am to you. I saw his blind eye and all."

Josiah had come home not one hour after Mr. Ratch ran off with the oxen.

"Josiah, wait until morning!" Ma ordered when my brother picked up his musket and stepped out the front door. "Even with the full moon, there's not enough light for tracking. It's much too dangerous to be in the forest at night."

Josiah's face was red and his jaw set. "He'll have them in the British camp by morning."

"It's a chance you must take," Ma said quietly.

"I'll go with you at first light," I offered. "You always say Mr. Ratch is lazy. Maybe he won't want to walk Goliath and Fred all the way to the British camp tonight."

Josiah stood his musket alongside the door. Ma had already hung Pa's gun on the pegs above the fireplace.

"You can't go with me, Annie," Josiah said. "You saw for yourself that Liam Ratch is not above killing children."

"I am not a child," I protested. "I am twelve years old, and I can track as well as you can."

Josiah smiled, but it was plain his mind was made up. I wasn't about to cry and prove to him that I was still a child, so I climbed the steep, narrow stairs to my room and lay down on my featherbed. Hot tears stung my eyes.

It had been an uncommonly hot and rainy summer, and this night would find sleep even harder to come by than usual. My cotton chemise and drawers stuck to my skin as I tossed and turned, running over in my mind all that was going on in that summer of 1777.

It was a tense time. At Sunday meeting, all the men talked about was war and independence. The Tories all said that when General Burgoyne's great army of Redcoats came marching down the valley all us rebels would get run off. Liam Ratch even boasted that he'd take over our land when we left.

The patriots, which were Josiah and Ma and all of us who wanted independence from the British king, vowed that no king's army was going to come marching through our farms, taking everything we had.

Through the summer, we saw more and more Continental troops riding through, traveling from Saratoga to Stillwater and Albany, and then back again. Ma said some came all the way from Massachusetts and New Hampshire. We saw less and less of our Tory neighbors as the summer went on. A few of them still showed up at Sunday meeting, but they were less boastful now. Most had already packed off to the north, bound for Canada. Some of them, Liam Ratch among them, stayed by to steal whatever they could from the valley's farms to supply the British and German armies that were coming our way across the great wilderness.

All of our neighbors had lost livestock that summer. Josiah kept Goliath and Fred in the pen near the barn instead of up in their pasture. He thought they were safe there. He never thought a Tory raider would steal them right out from under our noses, but Liam Ratch had done just that.

I stared at the ceiling long into the night, imagining Tories and soldiers and Indians lurking in the fields and forests that surrounded our farm.

Chapter 3:

Tuesday, August 19, 1777 –

When morning light finally seeped through the shutters on the small eyebrow window of my bedroom, I was sweaty and disheveled. I had slept some, but now I was wide awake. I pulled on my dress and rushed downstairs. Ma had a pot of mush on the cook fire.

"Where is Josiah?" I asked.

There was worry in Ma's blue eyes.

"He went out at dawn to look for Mr. Ratch and the oxen," she said.

"I wanted to go with him. I want to help him find Goliath and Fred."

"Annie, Goliath and Fred are not pets, and you must not think of them as such."

"I raised Goliath from a calf myself. He eats out of my hand. He comes to me when I call. Fred does, too."

"Put it out of your mind. It is Josiah's place to search out the thief who stole them. It is your place to milk the cow and feed the geese and chickens before breakfast."

The morning air was warming quickly after the brief coolness of the dawn, and the barn was dank. I sat on the three-legged stool beside Bella and squeezed her warm, rich milk into an oak bucket. I watched through the doorway for any sign of Josiah returning with the oxen, but he did not come. When I finished, I turned Bella out in the pasture and put the half-full pail of milk in the shallow spring.

"Why isn't he back yet?" I asked Ma when I went back into the house. "Josiah has been gone a long time. What if he doesn't find Goliath and Fred?"

Ma glanced out the open door. "We'll be hard put to get our wheat to the mill without the oxen to pull the cart. Nor will we be able to get a crop in come spring."

"I heard the old men at meeting Sunday last say that the army will take all the horses and oxen we have. How will anyone get a crop in come spring?"

Ma put a hand on my shoulder. "Josiah has taken up arms with the militia himself, Annie, and I reckon he will give Goliath and Fred over to the patriot cause if they're needed."

That gave me something to think about for sure. All this talk of independence and fighting for our rights sounded fine. When the talk came down to my brother going off to fight, maybe getting shot, and giving Goliath and Fred over to the patriot cause, it didn't sound quite so fine any more.

Ma seemed to read my thoughts. "We'll all have to make sacrifices, Annie. Nothing so important as independence can be gained if we won't give up what is dear to us to gain it."

A figure emerged from the woods above the pasture and strode swiftly down the hill toward us. It was Josiah, and he was alone.

Chapter 4 –

Wednesday, August 20, 1777

As Josiah downed a breakfast of mush and gravy, he told us that he had tracked Liam Ratch and the oxen to a stream on the other side of the ridge where the trail disappeared.

"I'll help you look for them when you've finished eating," I offered.

"You'll do no such thing, Annie," Ma said. "You will help me with the garden. Confronting Tory raiders is a man's job."

There was a sharp rap on the door. I ran and pulled it open.

"Good morning, Captain Landers," I said as the young man standing there tipped his tri-corner hat.

"May I talk to your brother, Annie?" he asked.

"Of course," I said.

William Landers was a captain in our local militia, a tall, slender dark-haired boy barely twenty years old. He was as ardent a patriot as Josiah.

He leaned his musket against the wall and stepped inside.

"Morning, Miz Blair," the captain said. "Sorry to intrude, Josiah, but it's important that you come to the village. General Schuyler rode down to the Sprouts yesterday. He is no longer in command of the Northern Army."

"But who will be in command?" It was plain to see that Josiah was not happy with this news.

"General Gates. General Schuyler has been called to Philadelphia to answer for the loss of Fort Ticonderoga."

"But why?" Josiah asked.

"The Continental Congress is angry with General Schuyler. They say he should not have given up the fort. He retreated from Fort Ann and Fort Edward and Fort Miller. The British keep coming, and Schuyler and his men keep retreating."

"But he has slowed the enemy approach," Josiah reasoned. "He's bought us time. He's blocked roads and destroyed bridges. He's made it difficult for the British to move on. Had he made a stand at Ticonderoga with his small force and been beaten, the British would already be in Albany."

Captain Landers shrugged. "It's out of our hands, Josiah. General Schuyler is gone, and General Gates is in command."

They stepped out into the hazy sunshine, shouldered their muskets and headed down the road toward the village. When would Josiah take time to look for Goliath and Fred?

"Annie, if your other chores are finished, go to the garden and pull weeds."

"I pulled a whole basket of weeds yesterday," I complained. "I want to go after Goliath and Fred."

Ma scowled. "I know you do, but you can't. And Josiah has other responsibilities. Go pull another basket of weeds."

The sun was already high in the sky, and mountainous thunderclouds loomed to the west. As I knelt in the warm damp soil and pulled fistfuls of redroot and lambs quarter from around the squash plants, I recalled the day Pa brought Goliath home.

It was a midsummer day just like this one when I was six. Pa had gone down to Stillwater with four hand-hewn beams for Squire Thomas's new barn. When he came back, a sturdy red bull calf was trailing behind the horses.

"Squire Thomas is short on coins," he explained to Ma, "so he offered me this fine calf. If we can get another, Ruth, we'll have a team of oxen in a few short years."

Ma wasn't too happy with the calf instead of money, but I sure was. Pa gave me charge of the frisky little animal. He dearly loved to chase me around the pen, and to be chased by me in return. He would eat clover from my hand, and when he finally curled up in the warm grass to take a nap, I would stretch out next to him and lay my head on his sleek red hide.

Pa was amazed at his rapid growth. "He's going to be a regular giant," he chuckled.

"I shall call him Goliath," I said, "after the giant in our Bible story."

True to Pa's prediction, Goliath grew. He was a massive animal by the time he was two, but very docile and easy to handle. It was about that time that Josiah brought Fred home.

He'd gone fishing up on Mill Creek and wandered farther than he planned. Hurrying to get home before dark, he took a shortcut across the field of a farmer named Fred Hazlett. The Hazlett cabin had burned a fortnight before, and the family packed up what few belongings they'd saved and headed south to Albany.

As Josiah passed near the barn, he heard a loud moo. Behind the barn, he found a yearling ox alone in a muddy pen. What thinking caused Mr. Hazlett to leave the animal behind with no forage was a mystery to us all. Perhaps he had intended to return for it, but he never did. Josiah brought the bony, half-starved ox home. He was a red brindle color, more white than red, dull-coated and scruffy.

Goliath took to him right away, although he bullied him fiercely. Within days, the newcomer was romping around the pasture behind him. By the time the cold winds of autumn swept in from the north, Fred, as Josiah called him, was fat and sleek, almost as tall, but not nearly as broad, as Goliath.

Pa and Josiah trained the oxen to pull a plow and a cart, and they became a fine team, much admired by our neighbors. Even though Josiah was just thirteen at the time, he handled the oxen with the skill of a grown man. It turned out that this was a good thing, for that autumn, Pa took sick and died.

Chapter 5:

Wednesday, August 20, 1777

It was near to sundown before Josiah came home. I waited for him near the King's Highway, and by the time he came into sight, I was really angry. The whole day was wasted, and Liam Ratch had probably already sold Goliath and Fred to General Burgoyne's army.

I ran down the road to meet him. "You were supposed to come back so we could go after Mr. Ratch," I said angrily, falling into step alongside him. "Now the sun is going down, and it is too late to go."

"Hold your tongue, Annie," Josiah retorted. He was half jogging toward the house, and I had to hold up my skirt and run to keep up with him.

Ma was waiting at the door. Her face was set in a frown as we approached her.

"What is it, Josiah?"

Ma had seen in Josiah's eyes what I had been too angry to notice. Josiah carried important news, I now realized, news more important than getting our team back, more important even than General Schuyler being relieved of his command.

"Captain Landers believes that we may make a stand, right here, well north of Albany."

Ma wrapped her apron around her hands and sat heavily on a wooden chair. "Fight here?"

"It makes sense, Ma," Josiah said, leaning his musket up against the cabin wall. He pulled up a chair and sat down.

"But why here?" I asked.

"The river valley above us and below us is wide, but here it is narrow. If we fortify the bluffs behind us, it will give us a great advantage as the British march south. Our men can mount cannon on the crest of the hills. We will stop them here."

"Oh, Josiah," Ma said, "I have great fear of war. There has already been too much killing."

"If we don't stop them, Ma, the soldiers and settlers who have already died will have died for no good reason. This must be our own country. We must be in control of our own destiny."

Josiah's passion was disturbing. I knew that he felt strongly about independence. It was plain that he was eager to march with the militia and take on the British and German armies that were slowly making their way toward us, but Ma was right. Every day there was news of more killings and scalpings. The whole Allen family, murdered at their dinner table a month ago on their farm near Salem. A day or two later, beautiful Jane McCrea, killed and scalped near Fort Edward by General Burgoyne's Indian scouts. Patrols, woodcutters, messengers . . . it didn't seem to matter if they were soldiers or militia, Tories or patriots, or just regular folks going about their business, all were in danger. And now Josiah was telling us that the fighting might take place right here in our own fields, along the peaceful and beautiful Hudson River.

We sat in silence, each of us lost in our thoughts and fears. Ma's eyes were misted with tears. I looked out the window at the hills that rose behind our house. Cannons up there? Surely it would never come to that.

Chapter 6:

Thursday, August 21, 1777

As I finished milking Bella the next morning, a large group of men stopped by the front gate. Josiah went out to greet them.

"Morning, Josiah."

Alden McGinnis, our neighbor to the south, came up the front path. His son John, who was but a year older than I, followed close on his heels. The other men sat in the grass, wiping sweat from their brows.

"Where are you all headed?" Josiah asked.

"Captain Landers tells me your oxen were stolen two nights ago."

Josiah nodded.

"So were mine."

"And both of my horses," said one of the other men.

"Six ewes, four lambs and a pig," chimed in a third. "And Squire Thomas's grist mill was raided, too."

"We've all lost livestock," Mr. McGinnis said. He lowered his voice. Did he think Tories were lurking nearby? "We know where they're hidden."

"Where?" Josiah asked.

"A lot closer than you might care to think," Mr. McGinnis said.

"Annie! Come in the house." Ma stood in the doorway, hands on hips.

"But, Ma. . ."

I glared at John McGinnis, who stuck his tongue out at me and grinned. Why must I go in the house, but he was allowed to stay there with the men?

I carried the milk pail into the oppressive heat of the kitchen. Ma had a cook fire going and bread in the brick ovens.

"You will not stand around and listen to man talk," Ma said sternly. "There is a bowl of beans on the table. Shell them and lay them out for drying."

Beans. Josiah and John McGinnis and the men were going after Tory raiders, and I was shelling beans. Why was I born a girl anyway?

I picked up a knife and hacked angrily at the stem ends of the beans, then slipped the pods open and pushed the beans out with my thumb onto a linen cloth. There was a tap at the door, and I turned to see John McGinnis standing there, his face red and his eyes puffy.

"Come in, John," Ma said with a smile. "What can I do for you?"

John looked at me, then at the floor. There was torment in his eyes.

"My pa . . ." he glanced at me again, then averted his eyes once more, ". . . wants me to stay here with you while they go after the Tory raiders. He says it's too dangerous for me to go."

"Why of course," Ma said. "You can help Annie shell beans."

I grinned at John and shoved the bowl of beans across the table so he could reach it.

We shelled beans, gathered the eggs from the henhouse, and stacked wood in the woodshed. John barely spoke as he worked alongside me. At noonday, Ma gave us boiled turnips and bread for our meal. Suddenly John stood up from the table and ran to the door.

"They're back!" he cried. "They have the cattle and horses!"

Ma and I joined him. Sure enough the tramping of hoofbeats and the bleating of sheep was getting louder. The men prodded more than a dozen cows and oxen and at least as many sheep and a few pigs along the rutted road. Mr. McGinnis drove a cart piled high with flour and grain sacks. Josiah and another man were riding the stolen horses.

"Hello!" Mr. McGinnis called out as Ma, John and I ran to the road. "We found them hidden in a ravine up on Mill Creek. The Tories ran off like rabbits when we came down the hills at them."

"Look at all the booty they gathered," Ezekiel Duffy said.

My joy was quickly turning to dismay. The cattle were milling in a circle in front of our house, but Goliath and Fred were not there. Josiah dismounted from a broad-backed dapple gray horse and handed over the reins to Mr. Duffy.

"Liam Ratch was among them," he said, "but Goliath and Fred were not there."

My heart sank. They had driven off the Tory raiders, but they hadn't found Goliath and Fred. Much as I tried, I couldn't stop the tears from streaming down my cheeks.

Ma put an arm around my shoulders. "Don't cry, Annie," she said softly. "It isn't seemly that you should cry in front of men who have risked so much."

I turned and fled to the back of the house where I could cry as much as I wished. Goliath and Fred would be pulling British cannons when the armies came to fight in our valley.

"You can borrow our oxen, Annie."

I looked up. John was standing beside me, his hat in his hands. "I know if we had not gotten our team back, I would feel just as you do."

"Did you raise yours yourself?" I asked. How could John McGinnis know how sad I was?

"Yes, I did. Pa gave me charge of them when they were small calves. I even helped Pa break them to the yoke, and this spring I pulled stumps with them myself."

Maybe John did know how I felt. "You have a fine team, too," I said. "Yours even look alike. I'm glad that your father was able to get them back."

"We will find Goliath and Fred, Annie."

I so hoped John was right.

A galloping horse thundered up the road. Its rider reined in and stopped where the men and livestock were gathered. There was hooting and laughter and shouts of "Hurrah!" John and I ran to see what the commotion was.

"There was a great victory at Bennington!" the mounted soldier was saying. "We have beaten Burgoyne's German allies badly. General Baum is dead. General Stark and his men took many prisoners, and chased the rest back to Fort Miller."

"Are our men still in pursuit?" Alden McGinnis asked. "Can we cut them off before they get back to Burgoyne?"

"That we don't know," the soldier said. His lathered horse pawed the ground.

I dipped a bucket of water from the spring and brought it to the men. John brought another and watered the rider's panting horse.

"Captain Landers wants you to come to Stillwater as fast as you can get there. The rider from Bennington will relate all the news to us as soon as he is rested."

The men talked among themselves, deciding how to disperse the recovered animals. Some had already been returned to their owners. Mr. McGinnis told John to put theirs in our stock pen. The rest would either be taken to their own farms along the way, or penned up near the village to be collected later, the men decided.

The cart lurched forward. Josiah remounted the grey horse.

"What about Goliath and Fred?" I asked, tugging at his boot.

Josiah's face was stern. "I don't know, Annie," he answered. "I have to go to the muster. If there is time before sundown, I will search for them again."

I watched Josiah ride off with the others. Ma turned and went back into the house.

"Put the oxen up and come inside," she said. "There's work to be done."

John and I drove their oxen up past the barn and into our empty stock pen. John put the gate bars in place. They were a fine team, but not nearly as handsome as Goliath and Fred, I told myself. They were rusty red, a shade darker than Goliath. John rubbed their heads and stroked their necks as they stood looking over the fence.

"What are their names?" I asked.

"Henry and George," John said laughing. "We named them after Pa's brothers."

I pulled an armful of hay from the pile and threw it over the fence. Henry butted George away from the hay and began eating.

"Henry is the boss ox," John said. "He'll let George eat after a while."

"Goliath pushes Fred around, too. But they always work together."

We left the oxen to their hay and went into the house. Ma was seated beside the table, her shoulders stooped and her head down.

"What is it, Ma?" I asked.

She wiped tears from her eyes as she turned and looked past us to the open door. Our field of shocked wheat spread out under the hazy August sky. Clouds loomed over the high mountain east of the river.

"They'll be even more desperate now," she said in a voice barely more than a whisper. "If they've been beaten in battle, they'll come at us with all they have left."

Chapter 7:

August 22, 1777

Mr. McGinnis and Josiah returned so late from the militia muster that Mr. McGinnis thought it wise to stay off the roads until morning. He and John bedded down in a corner of our parlor.

At dawn, as I went out to milk Bella, I saw Josiah and Mr. McGinnis ride away, to the north, in search of Goliath and Fred, I prayed. By the time I had turned the cow back into her pasture, two loaded carts had already rolled by the house, headed south on the King's Highway. Our neighbors were pulling up stakes and heading for the safety of the towns and villages. It seemed that everyone knew what Ma knew. The British and their German and Indian allies would be coming our way, in dire need of horses and cattle and everything else they could lay their hands on. I prayed that we would not choose to leave our house and farm to the British.

John had busied himself splitting wood in the cool of the early morning. He had a sizeable stack ready to go to the woodshed when Ma called to us to come and eat.

As I led John through the door, a two-wheeled cart clattered down the road, careening along behind a loping horse. It pulled up at our front gate and the driver leaped down. It was our neighbor from over the ridge, Nathaniel Trane.

"Beggin' your pardon, Miz Blair," he said, doffing his slouch hat. "My wife. . .the baby is coming, but she's having an awful time of it."

Ma was often called on to birth babies.

"Come along, Annie. You too, John."

Mr. Trane helped Ma climb up onto the cart and scrambled up into the driver's seat. John and I jumped up on the back. He turned the horse in a tight circle, and lashed it on its rump. The horse lunged forward. John and I held on tightly. Mud sprayed up from the wheels and spattered us as we bumped along the rutted road.

"How long has she been laboring?" Ma asked.

"All afternoon yesterday, and all the night long," Nathaniel Trane replied.

He was a young man, a few years older than Josiah, slight of build, blond and freckled. His wife was no older. They often came to Sunday meeting. She was the daughter of Fred Hazlett, the farmer who had abandoned his burned-out farmstead and his young ox three years before. They had put up a small cabin on the same site, and planted their first crop this past spring.

The horse loped along the road, mud flying up from the wheels of the cart. John and I clung to the sides. After several miles, we turned off the main road and traveled up a hill. The road led northwest in the direction a small settlement near the quaker's spring. As we climbed out of the river valley, Nathaniel turned up a narrow trail leading up a low ridge. Just before we reached the top, I stretched to see the turn-off that led to Liam Ratch's rundown cabin. It wasn't visible through the dense trees.

An idea seized me. I jumped from the cart. Startled, Nathaniel reined his horse in.

"Are you hurt, Annie?" he asked.

"My back hurts from bumping along," I said. "I'll walk the rest of the way. John will keep me company."

"It's too dangerous!" Ma protested.

"Mr. Trane's house is just over that rise. We'll be right along, Ma, I promise."

Ma looked at me, and I could see anguish in her eyes. I knew she was worried about Julia Trane and her baby, but all the talk of Indians and Tories skulking through the woods caused her constant fear.

"Please be watchful. And don't tarry."

John jumped off the cart. With a crack of the whip, the horse broke into a fast trot and the cart disappeared over the hill.

"My brother has already looked for Goliath and Fred at Mr. Ratch's cabin," I told John, "but if he had them hidden, he may be bold enough to bring them back now that Josiah has come and gone."

"You don't think he sold them to the British already?"

"Why didn't he have them with the other livestock in the ravine Josiah and your father raided yesterday? If he was going to sell them to General Burgoyne, they'd have been there with the others."

"My Pa said old man Ratch's family ran off to Canada weeks ago. No one has seen Mrs. Ratch all summer."

I turned down the path toward Liam Ratch's cabin. Insects buzzed around us, and the air was heavy. We walked quickly and quietly, ever scanning the forest on all sides of us.

I had been to Liam Ratch's cabin a few times. His children were sickly and Ma had come several times to tend them, had even helped with the birth of two of them. Poor Mrs. Ratch was a befuddled woman, poorly suited to cope with the wilderness, Ma said. Mr. Ratch had cleared but one small field, and they were surrounded by dense woodland.

As the clearing appeared through the trees, we left the trail and slunk behind trees and bushes. The cabin was a squat, square windowless building with a lean-to off one side. The door hung from a single hinge. There was no sign of Mr. Ratch or Goliath and Fred. I stopped behind a massive maple tree at the edge of the field. John knelt beside me, his eyes roving back and forth along the ground before us.

"Doesn't look like anyone's been here in weeks," he whispered.

"Let's go closer. Have a look for tracks."

We hastened across the clearing to the cabin. The whole place smelled. Their necessary was only a few feet from the cabin, and dried-up dung was piled in a corner of their stock pen. Rotten vegetables lay unharvested in the kitchen garden. It was a sad and dreary place.

"Look over here," John said.

He had walked around the back of the small barn.

"What did you find?"

"Cow tracks."

"Or ox tracks."

John pointed to the muddy ground. Sure enough, there were large cloven-hoofed prints milling about the area behind the barn. The prints were fairly fresh.

"Josiah told me Mr. Ratch's ox died this past spring. He didn't even plant a crop," I said.

I circled around the trampled area. At the north side of the clearing, the tracks became defined. Two sets of hoofprints led toward Liam Ratch's woodlot, and boot tracks as well. We followed them through the woodlot, down a steep path into a ravine and across a creek. We scrambled up the far side of the ravine into a small grassy clearing. Every now and then, John would raise his hand, motioning me to stop. Then we would stop and listen to the sounds of the forest. But we never heard any human sounds, or any movement other than the birds that flitted through the treetops.

We came upon a small marsh, and the tracks disappeared. John circled one way and I the other. At the opposite side of the clearing, I found the trail again. "Here, John," I called softly. "They went this way."

We continued to follow the tracks, winding away from the marsh and along a rough trail through giant white pine and hardwood trees. A deer bounded across the trail, startling us both. The trail continued in an eastward direction, twisting through the trees. We saw a farm in the distance, but the tracks seemed to keep well away from it.

"Your Ma is going to be angry with us," John said. We had walked at least a mile, and I wasn't even sure which direction the Trane farm was any more. The trail was so roundabout, I had lost all sense of direction.

"Where do you suppose he is taking Goliath and Fred?" I asked.

"Annie, you don't even know that it is Goliath and Fred," John complained. He sat down on a rock and pulled off his shoes.

"I am certain it's them. Look at the tracks. Goliath is much bigger than Fred. The left side prints are bigger. That's Goliath. And Fred has a chunk out of his right forefoot. See?"

John peered down at the tracks. "Yes, I see."

"He stumbled on a sharp rock last week. It cut a wedge out of his hoof."

"Have you even thought what we'll do if we catch up to them?"

"I will demand he return our oxen. He has no right to take them."

"He has your oxen, Annie. That is all the right he needs."

As angry as John's words made me, I knew he was right. I had heard the men at meeting laughing at how General Burgoyne's Indians stole horses from the Tories and then sold them back to other Tories. It seemed to be the way it was. If you could steal them, you owned them.

John put his shoes back on, and we started along the narrow path again. Where could Liam Ratch be going with Goliath and Fred? Was he going to all this trouble just to keep the oxen off the King's Highway?

The path dipped once more down a rather steep hillside. At the bottom, alongside a rushing stream, was a rude hut with holes rotted through the roof.

"A trapper's hut, maybe," John said quietly.

We moved slowly down the hill, careful not to make a sound. The back end of a two-wheeled farm cart was visible beyond the little building. Grazing alongside the stream, still yoked together, were Goliath and Fred.

Chapter 8:

August 22, 1777

"Where are you going?" John demanded as I pushed my way through the brush, down the hill toward the clearing.

"I am going to get Goliath and Fred."

John grabbed my arm and spun me around. "Don't be a goose, Annie! Liam Ratch would kill you as quick as he'd kill a snake."

Of course John was right. And I was sure Liam Ratch was in that awful hut.

"We'll wait until dark and sneak them away," I suggested.

"We don't even know which way to go, and once it gets dark we'll not be able to backtrack."

"We'll just follow the stream. That will take us to the river. All the streams run down to the river."

"It will be impossible to find our way in the darkness," John complained.

A bright flash lit up the sky, followed almost immediately by a loud clap of thunder. I hadn't even noticed the storm building.

"This is good, John."

We ducked under a newly-fallen white pine tree. Its wide branches would offer some shelter from the rain that pelted down.

"What's good? We'll be wet to the skin," John grumbled. "We're lost, and we will be soaked."

"We can take the oxen and get away. Liam Ratch will not come outside in this storm."

A gust of wind drove the rain right at us, shelter or no. Lightning flashed again, followed by another crack of thunder. I could see Goliath and Fred through the rain. They stood with their heads down and their backs to the wind near the back of the hut.

"I'm going to get them," I said.

"You'll be struck by lightning," John warned. "Wait until the storm moves on."

We huddled there, with the wind whipping the pine boughs around us, and the rain lashing at us. But it was a fast-moving storm, and soon the thunderclaps became a distant rumble. The wind let up, and the rain slowed down to a light, steady drizzle.

"Go now," John said, crawling out from under the tree.

I scrambled out of the shelter, and went out into the clearing. The oxen had gone back to grazing, and stood facing in my direction.

"Goliath!" I called softly. With my hand out, I walked toward him. Goliath raised his bedraggled head.

"Come, boy," I urged.

He twitched his ears, spraying rainwater around. I stooped and pulled up two handfuls of grass and held them out to him.

"Come on, Goliath. Come, Fred."

I stepped backward slowly, shaking the fronds of grass, as the oxen came toward me. I glanced at the hut. There were no windows. If luck was on my side, we would get away before Liam Ratch knew the oxen were gone. The cart was not covered. It was piled high with pots and kettles, harness and tools. It appeared he planned to make his escape before he sold our team to the British.

The oxen were almost within my reach. Goliath curled his long, pink tongue around the handful of grass I held out. I grabbed the end of the yoke and pulled.

"Stop right there. You ain't takin' these animals nowheres."

I felt something hard pressed into my spine, a gun barrel, I was certain, but the voice was not Liam Ratch's.

"They're mine, and I am taking them." I hoped I sounded braver than I felt.

"Pa said he paid you for them. They ain't yours no more."

There was a dull thud, a scuffle, and the gun barrel was suddenly gone from my back. I spun around to see John holding a musket trained on a ragged girl.

"Well, Lily Ratch," I said, "we've not seen you since spring. What are you doing holed up in this old hut?"

Her stringy black hair was plastered to her head, and her long, wet dress clung to her.

"Hidin' from all you rebel riffraff. All this war talk has made Pa edgy. He brought me this cart and these oxen and told me to get my sisters out of here."

John stood the gun on its butt as Lily's three little sisters, barefoot and scrawny, came out of the hut. The littlest one was no more than four, and the eldest of the three was eight, both with blue eyes and red hair. The middle girl, about six as I recalled, was as dark and serious as Lily. She hobbled along behind the other two. Her left foot was badly misshapen. Club foot, Ma called it. The child wore a braided rawhide cord around her neck hung with three catamount claws.

"You gonna shoot us all?" asked the smallest one.

"No," John said, "we wouldn't shoot you. But we're taking Josiah's oxen back."

"Your pa stole them," I told Lily. "He said he was selling them to the British."

"He's been stealin' and sellin' for the past two months," Lily said. "Ain't done us much good, until he brought me this team. He told me to pack up the cart get on up the river. We got family at Munro's Meadows. He said we could stay there with our uncle until the British take the valley."

I looked around. There was no garden, no chickens. It wasn't even a proper cabin.

"How long have you been living here?" I asked.

"Since Ma died."

I was stunned. "We never heard your ma died. I'm real sorry, Lily."

"Pa ain't got on well with the neighbors in a while. He thought it best we moved out, keep away from folks who don't believe as we do."

"Where is your pa now?" John asked.

Lily shrugged. "Said he had some stock to sell to the British. He brought me this team and said it was my duty to get this cart and my sisters over to Munro's Meadow. Told me to load up and get."

John looked at me. If the stock he had to sell was the stock our men had reclaimed this morning, then Liam Ratch would most likely come back soon. If Goliath and Fred were all he had left to sell the British, he'd be anxious to get them.

"Look, Lily," I said, "I'm real sorry about your ma, and I wish we could help you get to Munro's Meadow, but I am taking these oxen back to Josiah."

The rain had stopped, and rays of sun streamed through parting clouds. In spite of the brief, cooling rain, the air was as thick and heavy as before.

"Go on, take 'em then," Lily said, anger and resignation in her voice. "We'll get by. We always get by. We don't need no help from nobody."

What kind of man was Liam Ratch? What kind of man put it on his thirteen year old daughter to make her way through hostile country, through prowling Indians and two gathering armies, charged with the safety of three young children? I looked at Lily. She had a tough exterior, for sure, but in those eyes I saw the glimmer of the child she was, afraid for herself, for her sisters, and probably even for her pa.

The sun was low in the sky. Ma would be worried about us. If we were to get back to the Trane farm before full darkness, we had to get a move on. And I feared that Lily's pa would show up soon.

I looked at Lily's sisters' faces. They were filthy and so thin. Their round eyes were filled with tears as they looked back at me. They were all named for flowers, I knew. Lily, Rose, Gardenia and Daisy. My bouquet, Mrs. Ratch often said, smiling down at her ragged little girls at Sunday meeting.

They hadn't a chance if they stayed there in that hut. They'd be caught in the middle if Josiah was right and the Continental Army met the British and Germans right here in this valley. I looked at John. "How far are we from the river crossing?"

"There's a ford near General Schuyler's place, Annie, but that's a long way off," John replied.

"If we can get them to the King's Highway, Lily could go on up to the village and find someone to come for her sisters. We can't just leave them here."

"Pa said the British are going to build a bridge above Saratoga," Lily said. "They've left Fort Edward, headed south. Pa has a certificate of protection from General Burgoyne."

"Your sisters can ride on the oxen," I said to Lily. We'll take you as far as ford at General Schuyler's place."

Lily shook her head. "The girls will ride on the cart."

"We can't take the cart, Lily. It will slow us down too much."

Lily set her jaw and glared at me, her dark eyes fairly snapping. "Pa says I must bring the cart."

I looked at the heavily-loaded cart. For sure, the cart was worth almost as much as the oxen in these times, but it did seem that Mr. Ratch had a lot more kettles and pots than one family could need. Most folks buried their household goods when they were leaving home for a time. Dug them up when they returned. Why was Mr. Ratch, who surely was no farmer to begin with, so concerned about getting this cartload of goods out of the woods?

"Help me hitch Goliath and Fred to the cart." I tried to sound confident, but truthfully, I was really scared.

"You're going to help us get to Saratoga?" Lily put both hands on her hips and stared at me, disbelief in her face.

"There's going to be a battle, my brother says," I told her. "Every day more Continental troops come in. If you get caught in the middle of it, you won't have a chance. You need to get across the river as soon as you can. Seems like right now it's the river that divides us from them."

"Why would you help us? No one else in the whole valley will pay us any mind at all."

"It's not your fault your Pa's a Tory," I said.

"And it's not your fault your brother's a rebel," she shot back.

I stared at her. She was right. But right now, the rebel sympathizers had the upper hand, and she needed to get away.

"If we promise to help you get to the river crossing, will you promise to go without a fuss and let us take Goliath and Fred back home?"

For a moment, Lily just glared. Then she nodded. "Can I have my musket back? I'm a real good shot, and these woods are full of wild animals and Indians."

I knew that what she said was true. The Indians were leaving General Burgoyne's company in droves, Josiah had told me. And the nightly cries of wolves and catamounts was downright eerie. Could Lily be trusted? I looked at John. He shrugged.

"I reckon you can have it back, Lily. Just mind what you use it for."

John handed the musket back to Lily. We backed the oxen up to the draw bar and secured it to the yoke. The little girls went back into the hut, and came out with a pile of quilts. With Lily's help, they shoved the pile of bedding atop the cart. Gardenia was surprisingly nimble as she climbed up the side of the cart after Rose. Lily lifted Daisy up, and the three of them settled on the quilts, happy smiles lighting up their faces.

"Follow that path," Lily said, pointing to a barely visible opening in the forest on the other side of the creek.

I ripped a switch off a maple sapling, and prodded the oxen. They leaned hard into the yoke. The muscles of their hindquarters rippled with the effort as the cart began to move slowly forward. With a creaking and groaning, the heavily-laden cart lurched and swayed behind the straining oxen. They pulled it down into knee-deep water. It rocked and tipped precariously, the girls clinging tightly to the sides, as it was pulled over the rocky creek bottom and finally up the steep bank on the other side. I walked alongside Goliath, and John alongside Fred. We followed the barely visible trail through deep woods. Lily followed behind us, the musket cradled in her right arm.

It was rough going. Goliath and Fred strained mightily to haul the heavily-loaded cart up steep hills, around sharp curves, and through standing water in the low areas. Their hides glistened with sweat. As I walked along beside Goliath, my eyes never stopped roaming, side to side, watching. . . watching for Indians, wolves, bears, catamounts and Liam Ratch.

Chapter 9:

August 22, 1777

We moved northeast, on a trail that was surely taking us away from the Trane farm. I hoped we would find a road soon, because the sun was getting low in the sky. The cart lurched and tipped, and each time it leaned heavily to one side the girls shrieked and giggled, tumbling around atop the load, but clinging tightly to the sides.

I hadn't see Lily in a while. She had dropped back, and when we stopped to wait for her, she told us to go on ahead, she'd be along. Truthfully, I didn't know whether to trust her or not.

Finally we reached a cleared field, and made our way across. There was a small cabin on the far side.

"Do you recognize this place, John?" I asked. "Do you have any idea where we are?"

John shook his head. "I've never been up this way."

There were no livestock, no smoke from the chimney. Another neighbor who had pulled up stakes and moved to safety, I suspected.

A road, barely more than rutted cart tracks, ran alongside the field. Too soon, we were back into deep woods. Suddenly I heard a muffled shriek. As I turned, I was grabbed from behind, a strong forearm lodged against my throat. Goliath and Fred stopped. As I struggled against my captor, Rose screamed.

"Let me go! Lily! Help me!"

An Indian was on top of the cart. He had Daisy under one arm and Gardenia under the other. It seemed that he noticed Gardenia's twisted foot, for he quickly dropped her and grabbed hold of Rose.

"Unhand those children!" John yelled.

I continued to kick and thrash, trying to get free. Holding the girls tightly against his hips, the man on the cart leaped to the ground. Gardenia picked up a large ladle and swung it at his back.

John jumped into the fray, lashing at the man who held me, pummeling him with both fists. I was gasping for breath when a musket roared, and wood chips flew from the tree behind me. The man released his hold and jumped back. As I crumpled to my knees, he pulled his tomahawk from his belt and faced the cloud of smoke that swirled near a big tree not twenty feet from the cart.

Lily stepped out from behind the tree, raised the reloaded musket and pointed it directly at the head of the man who held her sisters.

"You leave them children go," she snarled, drawing a bead on the Indian. "Release them right now."

The man let Rose and Daisy slip to the ground. They ran to Lily. Gardenia balanced atop the cart, her ladle gripped tightly in both hands, ready to do battle. Oh, how I wished Josiah and Mr. McGinnis would come galloping over the rise. I struggled to my feet and backed away from the Indian, leaning against the cart. John picked up a stout stick and brandished it at the intruders.

"Food," said the first man. He lowered his tomahawk and motioned to the cart.

"Do we look like we got food?" Lily snapped.

"Give them something, anything," John hissed. "Give them a sack of beans and maybe they'll go away."

"Rose, get a jug of molasses from under the big pot." Lily ordered.

Rose clambered up the side of the cart. Digging into the piled up pots and pans, she pulled out a stone jar. She jumped down from the cart and handed it to the Indian. Both of the men were tall, lean and muscular. Their heads were clean-shaven except for the long top-knots that hung down their backs, and they wore just breechcloths and deerskin moccasins. Their faces were streaked with red and black. Canadian Indians, I was sure, the fearsome scouts who traveled with the British, not the peaceful Stockbridge men who fished along the river in the summertime, and sometimes came to our farm looking to trade.

The Indian held the jug over his head, looking at it intently. Then he smiled.

"Prob'ly thinks its rum," Lily muttered as the two men backed away from the cart, turned and disappeared into the woods.

"Thank you, Lily," I said. My knees were shaking something fierce. "I sure am glad you came back when you did."

"I been followin' behind," she said. "It ain't good to stick all together when you're in the woods. Pa says there ain't nobody we can trust."

"You can trust us, Lily," I said.

"I ain't sayin' you can trust me," she replied.

Her eyes were dark as coals and fierce as a catamount's. She was awful young to be filled with so much anger and mistrust, I thought.

"There's a farmhouse not too far from here," Lily said, pointing ahead. "We'd better put in for the night. Them Indians just might be back."

A few stars appeared in the pale blue sunset sky. Ma must be frantic by now, I thought, but Lily was right. It was not safe to be traveling at night.

The cart lumbered along the road for another half mile when we came upon the cabin and its small open stock shed. A candle burned dimly in the cabin's only window.

"Do you know the people who live here?" I asked Lily.

"It's an old widow woman," she answered. "She ain't quite right in her head, and she don't like us much."

"I'll ask if she can put us up for the night," I said.

I rapped loudly on the cabin door. John and the girls waited in the roadway.

"Who's there?" a voice called out from inside.

"My name is Annie Blair," I answered, leaning right up to the door. "We need shelter for the night. There are six of us. Can you help?"

Silence.

"Please. We're tired and hungry," I said. "We have small children."

The door opened a crack, and the silhouette of a stooped old woman with a halo of white hair appeared against the fireplace light.

"Are you thieves?" she asked in a shaky voice.

"No," I replied.

"Are you loyalists?"

I wasn't quite sure how to answer that. I looked back at Lily who stood in the shadows where the old woman couldn't see her. She shook her head.

"No," I said, "We're patriots."

"Take this." She stepped away from the door for a moment, then returned with a pan of warm johnny cake. "You can sleep in the shed. That thievin' loyalist Liam Ratch stole my cow, so the shed's empty. Be on your way at first light."

"May we build a fire?" I asked. "The little girls will be frightened in the darkness."

"Don't burn my shed down."

The door shut, and I heard a bar jammed against it.

"Your father stole an old woman's cow?" I asked Lily.

She shrugged, but did not answer. In the distance, a pack of wolves howled eerily. I waved to John to bring the cart over to the shed.

We unhitched Goliath and Fred and pulled the heavy yoke off their necks. Goliath found a small tree and rubbed his sweaty neck and head against the bark, pleased to be free at last from the heavy cart and the confining yoke. Fred butted him playfully, and the two came head to head, trying each to push the other back.

"What are they doing?" Daisy asked.

"Playing," I said. "Trying to see which of them is stronger."

"Like the soldiers," Rose mused. "Like the British and the Continentals."

I looked down at her serious face. Unlike Lily, she had very blue eyes and red hair. "Yes," I answered. "like the soldiers."

The oxen soon tired of their game and went to grazing in the clearing behind the cabin. As usual, Goliath, the bigger and stronger, had prevailed. Would the Continentals be bigger and stronger by the time they came head to head with the British army?

John built a small fire. After we had shared the johnnycake, Rose and Daisy curled up in a quilt and huddled against Lily. Lily held the musket across her lap.

Gardenia lay beside me on another quilt, her head on my knee. I stroked her dark hair back from her face.

"Where did you get that pretty necklace with the cat's claws, Gardenia?" I asked.

She fingered the glossy claws and smiled. "One of Pa's Indian friends gave it to me," she said. "He told me it is magic, and it will help me to run as fast as a catamount."

"That was very nice of your pa's friend to give you that," I said.

Gardenia smiled. "He is a very nice Indian."

The sky by now was a hazy mass of stars and the moon hung low over the hills to the east. Heat lightning flashed way off. A catamount screeched. I shuddered. John tossed another small stick into the flames, sending a shower of sparks into the night sky.

"How did your ma die?" I asked Lily. I felt the need to hear some sound other than that of predatory animals. I wondered anyway if those sounds were really animals, or were they Indians?

"She birthed another young 'un," Lily replied, "but it didn't go right. The babe was dead when we finally got it out. Ma bled to death before dawn."

A birth gone wrong. I felt a cold chill. Ma was right now at the Trane farm helping young Julia Trane give birth. And all the time frantic that John and I were kidnapped by Tories or Indians, or eaten by wolves.

"So it's fallen on you to be mother to your sisters," I mused.

"Mother and father most of the time. Pa's always off with the Tory scout findin' stuff to sell to the British."

"Why didn't you send for my ma when the baby was coming? She might have helped."

"Ma asked for her," Lily said quietly. "But my pa said it was your ma's fault that Gardenia's foot ain't right. Said your ma put a witch's spell on her."

I laughed, but there was no mirth to my laugh. "A witch's spell!" I said. "My ma is the furthest thing from a witch. She would never do anything to harm a child."

Lily glared at me with those fierce, dark eyes. "Pa says it's her fault Gardenia's a cripple."

I glared right back. "Gardenia is not a cripple," I said. "She just limps."

The stifling heat of the day was finally giving way to the pleasant coolness of night. I pulled the quilt over Gardenia's shoulders.

We sat in silence. One by one, the girls fell asleep. The rhythmic sound of their breathing was soothing. Katydids and crickets chirped, and an occasional owl hooted. I knew that a lot of families slept out in the woods at night during the warm seasons, feeling safer in the open than in the confines of a cabin with a single door. But how I wished I was at home in my room.

Soon John was asleep, too, but Lily remained watchful, the musket still cradled in her arms.

"Why don't you sleep?" I asked. "I'll watch for a while, then you can spell me."

"Most nights I don't sleep at all. It ain't safe to sleep."

I felt pity in my heart for Lily, but great respect as well. She was not yet fourteen years old, but she carried burdens that would fell a grown woman. She wouldn't sleep, I knew. I lay down on the dirt floor and closed my eyes, protected through the long and perilous night by Liam Ratch's daughter.

Chapter 10:

Saturday, August 23, 1777

It was still dark when John shook me awake. Goliath and Fred lay nearby, chewing their cuds. Lily had a rabbit carcass on a spit over the small fire in front of the barn. It smelled heavenly.

"How did you get the rabbit?" I asked as I yawned and stretched.

"I set a snare," John said.

We all six shared a breakfast of rabbit, which wasn't much. Daisy, being the youngest, got first pick and pulled off a back haunch. She ate it greedily. By the time it got around to John, there was almost nothing left.

"I'm not hungry anyway," he lied, handing the last of the portions to Lily.

Lily shrugged, and picked the bones clean. By then, pink light spread over the hills to the east.

"I split that pile of wood for the old lady in the house," John said.

The pile was neatly stacked by the cabin door. I was grateful that she'd allowed us to stay in her shed, and glad that John had done a good turn for her kindness.

John prodded the oxen to their feet. We hefted the yoke onto their necks and fastened it, then hitched the cart up. The girls piled on, and we set off down the road at a slow ox pace as the sun broke over the mountain. Mist hung low in the surrounding woods, which made me nervous. Was Liam Ratch lurking there? Or the Indians?

Lily dropped back out of sight again, protecting our rear, I hoped. I wasn't sure I liked having Lily walking behind me with a loaded gun, but not having her there was even more frightening.

"How long will it take us to get to the river?" I asked John after we had traveled for several miles. We came to a fork in the trail, and prodded the oxen to the east branch.

"We should be there by noonday."

The sun had burned off the mist, and the air was stifling. Mosquitoes buzzed around our heads, and flies troubled Goliath and Fred something fierce. They continually bobbed their heads, twitched their ears and swished their tails.

"John," I said in a low voice so the girls wouldn't hear me, "what if we meet British soldiers or Tories? Will they take us?"

John shrugged.

"And what if we meet patriot soldiers or militia? Will they take Lily and her sisters?"

"The Indians frighten me more than either the British or the militia," John said glancing around as if he expected a few more to leap from behind the trees. "They'd take any and all of us if they could, and these oxen as well."

At last we came out of the woodland into an area of open fields on hills that sloped downward. The river was a silver ribbon winding through the valley that opened up before us. What danger had we gotten ourselves into, offering to help Liam Ratch's daughters? It looked peaceful enough, but the valley was anything but peaceful.

The sun was high overhead, and mountainous thunderclouds were massing over the hills behind us when we reached the King's Highway.

A man and woman leading a stout horse with five children trailing behind it lumbered toward us from a southward direction. Tories, I was certain, since the word was that the British and Germans were nearing the village from the north and the Contintentals and militia were massing to the south.

"We could leave your cart here, Lily," John suggested. "These folks must be loyalists. You could travel with them."

Lily snorted. "I ain't leavin' this cart. If it was to get stolen before my pa got back for it, he'd be in a fine rage."

"Maybe they could hitch their horse up."

"That one horse is already as loaded down as a horse needs to be. He'd never pull this load. The oxen are havin' enough trouble in this muck."

The family pulled abreast of us and stopped. The man doffed his hat and wiped sweat from his brow.

"Hallo," he said. "Where you young folk headed?"

"We're hoping to make a river crossing at Saratoga," John said. "You headed that way, too?"

"We're going to the British camp for protection. I heard they're at Fort Miller."

"That's what we hear, too," John agreed.

"Is it true there are ten thousand colonials between here and the Sprouts?" the man asked.

"More every day, we hear."

"And a new commander who won't run?"

John nodded solemnly. "That's what we hear, all right."

The man's children had all sat down on the roadside. They were as bone-weary as we were, I reckoned.

"Then we'll keep on movin'. Good luck to you. Come along, children. There's a long ways to go yet."

The children struggled to their feet without a word of complaint and fell in behind the horse. Soon they were out of sight.

"How far is Fort Miller?" Lily asked. "Are you certain that's where the British are?"

"That's what the men were saying at the last militia meeting I went to," John said.

"You go to militia meetings?" Lily asked, her brow furrowed. "You're not old enough to join the militia."

John grinned. "No, but my pa is in the militia, and when he goes in to the meeting, I sit outside under the window and listen to what the men are talking about."

We headed north. Goliath and Fred plodded evenly along, following the road to Saratoga. Though it was called the King's Highway, the reality of it was that the road was rutted and narrow, just a bit better than the single track roads that led to the valley's scattered farms.

The stench of animal dung and wet muck hung heavy in the August air. Flies buzzed everywhere. Lily's sisters perched on the cart, scratching and squirming, but they gave not a word of complaint.

We soon came to a large clapboard farmhouse sitting on a side hill overlooking a wide cove in the river.

"This is the place they call Dovegat," John said. "Pa brought me here hunting this past spring. The house belongs to a colonel in the Continental Army."

"Josiah has spoken of it," I said.

It was a beautiful area. The wide expanse of placid water had an air of serenity. Geese and ducks swam along the shore, feeding in the shallows.

"Annie," Gardenia called, rising to her knees, "have you ever seen so many ducks?"

"There surely are a lot of them," I answered.

"Can we catch one?" Daisy asked. "Lily could make duck soup."

"They're too pretty to be duck soup," Gardenia said, glaring at Daisy.

"But I am so hungry," Daisy said plaintively. "I want duck soup."

"Hush, Daisy," Rose said. "We must move on."

The road curved past the big house and up a steep hill.

"You girls climb down from the wagon," Lily said. "Give these oxen a lighter load on this hill. You all can walk a ways."

The three girls clambered down, seeming happy to be free of the bouncing cart even for a little while. Rose and Daisy hopped along, jumping over ruts and puddles. Gardenia hobbled gamely along beside Goliath, sloshing through the mire. She reached out to pet his sweaty red hide.

"He's a pretty ox," she said. "His hair is red like Rose and Daisy."

I laughed. "Yes. And when Rose and Daisy are old, their hair will be all red and white just like Fred's is."

Gardenia hung back to get a look at Fred. "Is he a very old ox?" she asked.

"No, Gardenia, that's just his brindle coloring. He is younger than Goliath."

"He is pretty, too."

She came alongside me, and slipped her hand into mine. It was a struggle for her to even keep up with the slow oxen with her twisted foot.

"Would you like to ride pick-a-back?" I asked.

"I can carry her," John said.

"I don't need to be carried," Gardenia said defiantly. "I can walk."

"Of course you can walk," John said, "But I think you should be a fine general and I will be your noble horse."

Gardenia giggled at that. John squatted low, and she climbed up on his back. Making a great show of prancing and snorting, John circled the cart with Gardenia clinging to his back.

As we gained the crest of the hill, a line of a dozen or so militiamen came toward us.

Lily ducked quickly into the trees out of sight.

"Will they shoot us, Miss Annie?" Daisy asked, her voice tremulous.

"Of course not, Daisy."

Gardenia slid down from John's back, and the three girls hid behind us. As the men approached us, I wondered about the family we had met on the road. Had the militia let them pass without a challenge?

The men were clad in a ragtag assortment of uniforms and farmers' garb. They did not look terribly military, but their muskets were shouldered and their line was almost straight. The man in front raised his right hand and the column halted before us.

"Where are you headed?" he asked.

"Saratoga," John replied.

Several of the men walked around the cart, looking intently at the goods piled in it.

"Don't you know that the British army is camped just north of Saratoga? You're not loyalists, are you?"

"No, sir," John answered "We have kin in the village."

"You got a lot of kettles and tools here. Seems like too many for kin. You aren't taking this to the British camp, are you?"

"No, sir."

"Who are your kin?"

"My papa is Liam Ratch," Gardenia announced, peering around me. "He's a . . ."

"You children hush!" I scolded loudly. "You should not speak to an officer. Ma would be appalled at your lack of manners!"

"But I . . ."

"Hush, Gardenia! Not another word!"

The man seemed to puff up just a little at the reference to him being an officer. I held my breath.

"You aren't loyalist, are you?" he squinted as he looked from John to me.

I caught a slight movement in the brush alongside the road. I knew it must be Lily with her musket aimed at the man's head.

"No, sir!" John retorted. "My pa is Lieutenant Alden McGinnis with the militia in Stillwater. Annie's brother is Josiah Blair, also with the militia."

The man doffed his felt slouch hat and ran his fingers through his wet hair. "I know them both."

"Are you headed to Stillwater?" I asked.

"We are."

"If you see his pa or my brother, will you tell them we'll be home as soon as our errand in Saratoga is finished?"

He clapped his hat back on his head and saluted smartly. "Glad to. Be on you way, but don't linger in the village. It's a dangerous place for young folk."

The men marched away, their shoes making sucking sounds in the wet muck. I prodded Goliath on his rump and the cart creaked and groaned as it resumed its forward motion.

I felt Lily's presence over my left shoulder. I looked back at her, and her stare was chilling.

"You're a clever girl, Annie Blair," she snarled. "You'd best get those oxen moving. I'd hate to have your brother or his father show up before we reach the river crossing."

Chapter 11 -

Saturday, August 23, 1777

It was mid-afternoon when we came upon General Schuyler's country house and mills. Continental soldiers were camped on the grounds, but there were loaded carts nearby. It appeared that they were preparing to leave also. The men at Sunday service had often complained bitterly that the Continental Army seemed to be in a constant state of retreat. How were we to stop the British advance if we kept running, they wanted to know.

Lily had caught up to us as we passed the linen mill, the ever-present musket cradled in her arms. Several of the soldiers waved to us. We nodded in their direction but did not stop. A bridge spanned Fish Creek just past the mill. The water rushed over rocks, hurrying to the river. The planks rattled under the cart's wheels as we crossed. The ruins of old Fort Hardy stood near the river.

"Lily, I'm hungry," Daisy complained.

"So am I," Gardenia chimed in.

"The village is just ahead," Lily told them. "We will find something to eat there."

Soon we came into the small settlement. Few people were on the street, and it appeared that most of the houses and shops were abandoned.

"The oxen need to rest," I told Lily. "While John tends to them, you and I can look for something to feed these children. There must be kitchen gardens behind these houses."

"There is a ford back there near the old fort," John said. "We should try to cross the river there. At least Lily and her sisters will be on the same side as the British. Then we can go home."

Lily glared at John.

"He's right, Lily," I said. "We can't keep going right into the British camp. We'll get you across the river, but then we must go home. To keep going north is too dangerous."

Lily ran her fingers along the barrel of her musket. I had the chilling feeling that she was about to take the oxen from us anyway. She had given us her word, but was her word worth more than her father's was?"

"The girls are starving," I said. "Let us see what we can find for them to eat while the oxen rest."

Lily's dark glare of suspicion unnerved me. What kind of life had she had that she trusted no one? And yet, here I was, about to abandon her to her fate, with no real assurance that she and her sisters would get safely to their relatives in the hills to the east.

I helped John release the draw bar from the oxen's yoke. He drove them to a water trough that stood alongside the road in front of an apothecary shop.

I took Gardenia's hand and led her around to the back of the shop in search of a garden. Rose and Daisy skipped along behind us. I saw Lily look from the cart to us and back to the cart again. She seemed unsure whether or not to follow.

The yard behind the apothecary shop looked to me like the Garden of Eden. Butterflies and moths flitted about, and the air was tinged with the delicate scent of mint and lavender. An arbor hung heavily with green grapes stood to the rear of the garden. The garden itself appeared to have been neglected for some time. Squash, beans and potato plants sprawled in a tangle. Daisy ran to the arbor and pulled down a cluster of grapes. She popped several in her mouth, but quickly spit them out.

"They're sour!" she cried.

"Of course they're sour," Lily said. "They're not ripe yet."

We pulled up potato plants, digging the plump tubers from the soft earth with our hands. We stripped beans from their stalks. Rose even found some turnips. We filled our skirts, and soon had picked as much as four of us could carry, for Lily had disappeared again. Gardenia's cheeks bulged out like a chipmunk's as she chewed a mouthful of raw beans.

"Can we make a fire, Annie?" Rose asked. "Can we roast the potatoes? And some squash, too?

A raucous squawking startled me. Lily sprinted towards us from behind a nearby barn, two fat red hens dangling from her free hand.

"That old lady will never miss them," she said as she ran past me. "She's got a dozen of them. Come on, girls."

Rose and Daisy ran after Lily, holding tight to their bulging skirts. Gardenia gripped my arm with one hand, holding her skirt with the other, and pulled me toward the street. I looked back over my shoulder. A white-haired woman was bent over her garden behind a nearby cabin, hacking at weeds with her hoe. It seemed she had not heard the squawking of her hens, and was not aware that Lily had just stolen two of them. Deaf, I supposed, and defenseless against those who would take advantage of her. It was disturbing that the need to survive would turn us all into thieves.

I followed Gardenia around the shop. I had nothing to offer the woman in return for the hens anyway. As we came out onto the street, I stopped still in my tracks. John lay in the street beside Goliath, writhing in pain. Standing over him was Liam Ratch.

"What has happened? John, are you all right?" I glared at Liam Ratch. "What did you do to him?" I demanded.

I dropped the vegetables to the ground and ran to John's side. A few men had gathered, but no one was making a move to help John.

"Little sneak was tryin' to steal stuff off my cart," Ratch said. "I caught him red-handed."

"You're a liar!" I snapped, kneeling in the mud beside John. His right leg was grotesquely twisted.

"Insolent girl," Ratch snarled. "Call me a liar, will you?" Ratch glowered at me, his good eye squinted.

The men walked away. They were not interested in our dispute with Mr. Ratch. It occurred to me that they probably knew Liam Ratch, knew what he was, and did not want any part of his dealings.

"Please, Mr. Ratch," I said as calmly as I was able, "we've brought your girls this far. Help me put John on one of the oxen so we can go home."

"You'll go where I say, missy, and that sure ain't home. And you surely ain't gettin' either of these oxen."

Gardenia, Rose and Daisy had gathered around their father. Lily stood back, ever the guardian, watching.

"Get up on the cart. We're movin'out." Ratch lifted his daughters up over the side, then he grabbed John by one arm pulled him to his feet. John cried out with the pain, but Ratch paid him no mind. He shoved him up onto the loaded cart. John was sprawled face first on the pile of quilts. His hair was soaked with sweat, and his ears were bright red.

"Lily, you watch my back. You, girl, help me hitch this team to the cart."

Ratch backed Goliath and Fred up to the cart, and I helped him hook the drawbar to the yoke.

"You walk right alongside that ox so's I can see your every move," he ordered. He snapped Goliath with his prod, and the cart lumbered up a narrow street that led west out of the village. Lily handed the hens up to Rose and Daisy, who wrapped their arms around the struggling birds and held them fast. Then Lily dropped back, the gun cradled in her arms, watching.

The rocking motion of the cart caused John to moan. There was nothing I could do to help him, or myself.

We moved northwest away from the village. I knew that the way to the British camp was north along the King's Highway. I wondered where Liam Ratch was taking us. We had not gone very far when he turned the oxen into the dooryard of a burned out shell of a cabin.

Rose and Daisy scrambled down from the cart. I lifted Gardenia to the ground. John lay curled into a ball, not moving. Ratch unhitched the oxen from the cart, unyoked them and turned them loose on the grassy slope of the hillside behind the remains of the cabin.

"What you all got there for us to eat?" Ratch asked his daughters.

"Squash and beans, Papa," Gardenia answered.

"And potatoes," Daisy said.

"Turnips, too," said Rose.

"Good. Build us a fire."

"What about John?" I asked. "He can't stay up here."

Ratch looked up at John, and he grinned a toothless, mirthless grin. "For sure he ain't goin' to run. You goin' to run off without him?"

He grabbed John's good foot and pulled him over the side, catching him under the armpits before he hit the ground. John's face was ashen and tears streamed down his cheeks.

"I got some business with the Indians, Lily," Ratch said to his eldest daughter. He glanced at me. "She won't run, will she?"

"She won't leave John," Lily replied. "She'll stay."

Mr. Ratch helped John to a shady spot beneath a tree and eased him to the ground. John trembled violently.

"You ain't much good to anyone with that foot, boy," he said. He knelt down by John. "Get behind him and hold onto him," he ordered me. "I'll fix him right up."

I slid in behind John's shoulders and wrapped my arms around his chest. Ratch grabbed his foot and yanked it hard. John screamed, but the bone snapped back into place, his leg no longer bent at a right angle. Ratch pulled a length of cotton cloth from the bedding piled on the cart and ripped off several strips. With two straight sticks, he splinted the leg.

"Lily'll find you something to use for a crutch. I'll be back before dark."

With that, Liam Ratch disappeared into the woods.

Lily built a fire. She pulled a large kettle off the back of the cart, and soon had water boiling. She had killed one of the hens, and was busy plucking feathers off it.

John closed his eyes and appeared to doze. I helped Lily scrape and cut up potatoes and squash and threw them into the boiling kettle with the hen.

"Lily," I said "are we far from the river crossing?"

She shook her head.

"Then why don't you let us take Goliath and Fred and go home? You'll be able to find someone to help you get your cart to Munro's Meadows from here. Or maybe your pa could go over there and borrow a team of horses from your kin."

Lily looked at me and laughed. "You think I'm an idiot, don't you? I know what these oxen are worth. I know what you're worth, and him, too." She nodded in John's direction.

Her words chilled me to the bone, in spite of the stifling August heat. Now I knew where Liam Ratch had gone. Business with the Indians meant trading us. The Indians would pay well for white captives, just as the British would pay well for a fine team of oxen.

CHAPTER 13

Saturday, August 23, 1777

Lily took her axe and musket and went into the woods to cut a crutch for John. I sat beside him against the trunk of the tree. Rose and Daisy ran in circles, laughing as they played a game of tag. Gardenia hobbled after them falling occasionally, but laughing as hard as they were.

"What happened back there, John?" I asked. "How did your leg get broken?"

"Mr. Ratch pulled me off the wagon, and I caught my foot under the rail. My leg just snapped."

He grimaced, rubbing the side of his thigh. Sweat dripped from his forehead.

"I know why he won't let Lily leave the cart behind," he said in a low voice.

"Why?"

"When you were in the garden, I climbed up on the cart to see what it was he had under all those kettles and tools and harness. Didn't seem likely he'd make Lily risk so much for some kettles and tools and harness when the wise thing would be to get away as quickly as they could."

"What did you find?"

"Gold."

"Gold? You found gold?"

John nodded. He glanced around, but Lily was not in sight. "There was a loose floorboard in the front corner of the cart. It popped up when I stepped on it. There's a false floor in the cart. Underneath it, Mr. Ratch has a leather sack filled with gold coins."

In spite of the late afternoon heat, a cold chill raced up my spine.

"Gold," I said slowly. "So when Mr. Ratch gets this cart over to the British camp, he will sell the cart and the goods in it, he will sell Goliath and Fred, he will sell us to the Indians, and he will take his sack of gold coins and his four daughters and he will flee to Canada, a very wealthy man."

"Yes, he will."

"And he doesn't really care if the British win the coming battle or not."

"No."

Stealing from neighbors and old women and no doubt millers and shopkeepers and anyone who was not vigilant. Not a patriot and not a loyalist either. Just a common thief, a man without honor.

Lily came out of the woods carrying a forked stick. "Try this," she said.

I helped John to his feet, and Lily placed the crotch of the stick under his arm. He grimaced with the pain, but he was able to hobble a few steps.

"It'll do," he said.

It was near to dark when Liam Ratch returned. We had all eaten a fine dinner of the chicken stew Lily had made.

"Did you make your deal, Pa?" Lily asked, handing him a plate.

"Tomorrow at midmorning we'll cross at the ford. The Indian scouts'll meet us there. They'll deal. Then we'll go on to Munro's Meadow."

Ratch squatted near the fire, gulping down his meal like a wild animal. I thought hard about his answer to Lily. The Indians would deal. He would take his girls to Munro's Meadow.

Josiah had said that Burgoyne's Indians were deserting him in large numbers, going back to Canada. It was a known fact that they often took white captives, mostly women and children old enough to work. The Indians we had encountered the day before had clear intentions of taking us captive. Would Ratch trade us for goods, or for protection so he could safely reach Canada? My mind raced, trying to think of a way to escape, a place to hide. How could we run with John's broken leg?

"Can you get around with that crutch, boy?" Mr. Ratch asked John.

"Yes, sir," John answered.

"Good," said Ratch. "Then hop on over here and I'll fix you up for the night. Rose, bring one of them quilts from the cart."

Rose climbed up the side of the cart and retrieved one of the ragged quilts from the pile in the front of the cart. Ratch walked out behind the cabin, motioning for us to follow. I held John's free arm as we made our way into the deep shadows away from the fire. Rose followed, dragging the quilt along the ground. Mr. Ratch bent down in the darkness. There was a creaking noise, and he pulled up a wooden door.

"Here you go. Roof over your heads and all," he said.

I looked into the gaping blackness of a root cellar. Terror shook me.

"No," I said. "please don't put us down there. It looks like a grave."

"Don't worry," he laughed, his high-pitched cackling laugh, "I'll let you out come morning. I ain't takin' no chances on that fine team of oxen disappearing during the night, or you, neither."

He shoved me into the opening. I stumbled on the uneven wooden steps and barely managed to catch myself as I slid down into the root cellar. John screamed in agony as he fell headlong, his crutch bouncing off my shoulder. He hit the floor with a thud. The quilt followed, draping over my head. Angrily, I tossed it off. The door swung shut, obliterating the dim moonlight that shone above us and leaving us in total blackness. There was a loud clunk as Ratch secured the door.

John howled. I could not imagine the pain he was feeling. I groped around the cellar. It was constructed of fieldstone, a little wider than my height. A pile of oak baskets stood in the corner, empty. The floor was damp, and the place had the rank, musty odor of damp earth and spoiled vegetables. I climbed up the stairs and pushed against the door. It wouldn't budge.

Discouraged, I dropped back into the cellar. "Here, John," I said, spreading the quilt on the floor. "Lie here and try to sleep."

John dragged himself onto the quilt. I sat cross-legged, leaning back against the cold stones, and he laid his head in my lap. I looked up at the thin lines of moonlight that shone through the wooden door above. We were trapped. Trapped like rats.

CHAPTER 14 –

Sunday, August 24, 1777

John was feverish, and dozed fitfully through the night. Toward morning, a thunderstorm rumbled through, and the rain that seeped through overhead door soaked the quilt and left puddles on the floor. I heard every sound in the night. I could hear the tramping of Goliath and Fred as they grazed above the root cellar. Wolves howled, owls hooted, rain pattered. Daisy cried, afraid of the wolves or protesting the rain. I could hear Lily murmuring to her, calming her fears.

After hours of comfortless blackness, a shaft of light appeared in the spaces between the boards in the wooden door above us. There was the crack of an axe splitting wood. Soon I smelled wood smoke and knew that Lily had started a fire. I was growing very hungry.

I slipped out from under John's head and climbed up the stairs. I strained my ears to hear the low sounds of conversation between Mr. Ratch and Lily.

"I'll be goin' down to the ford now and see if them Indians has showed up," Ratch said. "Don't let those two out of the cellar until I get back."

"Yes, Papa," Lily answered.

The fading sound of footsteps let me know that Liam Ratch was off on his mission, a mission that may very well have John and me on our way to Canada with the Indians.

"What do you hear?" John asked, groggy.

"He's gone. Lily's cooking breakfast."

"Burnt turnips. I smell them," John complained.

The light was growing rapidly brighter. A shaft of sunlight streamed through the cracks, bathing our prison in soft light.

"John! There's a rat!"

John rolled sideways as a rat scurried behind a basket. He moaned with the pain of movement. "Kill it!" he cried.

"With what?"

"My crutch, you goose!"

I picked up the crutch and knocked the basket sideways. The rat ran toward my feet. I raised the crutch and brought it down hard, but I missed the rat. It disappeared into a hole in the stones. I stood shaking, and great tears rolled down my cheeks. I could see John's face in the light. He smiled.

"We're about to be sold to Indians, and you're crying over a rat," he said.

There was a loud grating sound, and the overhead door swung open. Lily was silhouetted against the bright sunrise.

"What's the racket down there?" she demanded.

"Annie was doing battle with a rat," John said, "but the rat won."

"You should have killed it," she said. "Rats aren't bad eating when you got nothing else."

The thought of eating a rat made me cringe. Had Lily really eaten rats?

"Come on up here," she ordered.

I helped John climb the stairs. Lily took his crutch from me and steadied him as he stepped out of the root cellar. She adjusted the crutch under his arm. I went back down for the quilt, dragged it up the stairs and spread it on a big rock to dry in the sun. John hobbled toward the fire.

"Listen, Annie," Lily whispered as I started toward the fire, "why don't you and John just head off into the woods before my pa gets back?"

I stopped in my tracks and stared at her. Was she really offering to let us go?

Goliath and Fred grazed nearby.

"John can't travel on foot, Lily. We wouldn't even make it back to Fish Creek."

"What are you sayin'?"

"I need the oxen. If we are to escape, John must ride. Please, Lily."

She scowled darkly. The three little girls were sprawled side by side on a pile of quilts under the cart. Rose rolled over, but did not wake up.

"My pa will whip me good if I let you get away with one of them oxen."

I took a deep breath. "Not one, Lily. Both. They're a team. A right hand and a left hand. One needs the other."

"Are you mad, girl?" Lily hissed.

"No. You know it's right. You know that your pa stole them. You know that he's going to sell us to the Indians. And you know that we can't get away without the oxen."

Lily turned and walked away from me. She leaned down under the cart and covered Rose with a quilt. Gardenia raised her head. Lily stroked her hair and murmured to her softly. Gardenia looked over at me, smiled and crawled out from under the cart. She lifted the cat's claw necklace over her head and held it out to me.

"Here, Annie," she said. "This will help you to run as fast as a catamount."

"Thank you, Gardenia." I knelt down before her and embraced her wiry little body. "Lily is very fortunate to have you by her side."

Gardenia hugged me, then crawled back under the wagon. I slipped the necklace over my head and glanced anxiously toward the river. There was no sign of Liam Ratch, but I knew it wouldn't be long before he came back.

Lily stood facing me. There were tears in her eyes.

"All these years we lived in this valley, not one person ever treated us decent. Only your ma. And now you. Why? Why would you pay mind to a passel of no-account Ratch children? Why would you risk your life to bring us here? Back at the hut, all you had to do was take your oxen and go home. Why didn't you?"

I looked at the proud, scrawny girl who stood before me. . . the girl who had helplessly watched her mother die in childbirth . . . who had taken over the rearing of her motherless sisters, and who had stood up to Indians in defense of those little sisters. . .the girl who would defy her father to let us get away.

"Lily Ratch," I said, "you have more courage than anyone I've ever known. My ma says we all have to make sacrifices if we are to hold on to what is dear to us. I reckon you've already made more sacrifices in your life than most folk ever will."

Lily rubbed her eyes and turned away. "Take your oxen and git before my pa comes back."

"You'll be all right, Lily. Your pa will find a way to get you all safely to Munro's Meadow."

How I hoped that I was right.

I brought Goliath and Fred to where John stood near the fire. The three of us lifted the yoke up and fastened it to their necks. Together, Lily and I hoisted John up onto Fred's broad back.

"Godspeed, Lily," I said. "And thank you."

I motioned Goliath forward and the team lumbered up the hill away from the road. We would find our way through the woods, around the village and the farms, and hope that we could find General Schuyler's home before Liam Ratch found us. I prayed that the Continental soldiers were still there.

CHAPTER 15 –

Sunday, August 24,, 1777

The trail through the woods was rough. We dodged low-hanging limbs and stepped over roots and rocks. Through the tree-tops, I noticed the darkening sky closing in on the bright morning sun. It seemed like it had rained nearly every day that summer.

John clung to Fred's back, lying low to avoid the punishing limbs. I knew he must be suffering something awful, but we had to make haste. Liam Ratch would be hard on our trail when he discovered us missing.

What would he do to Lily, I wondered. I hoped he would not be too harsh with her.

"Do you know where we're going, Annie?" John asked.

"Fish Creek is to the south. We must go west to get away from the King's Highway, then turn toward the south to reach the creek. If good fortune is on our side, there will be soldiers camped near the creek at General Schuyler's farm."

Mosquitoes and flies harassed us without mercy. Goliath and Fred tossed their heads constantly, trying to rid themselves of the annoying insects. With every lurch and bump, John's grimace grew more strained.

As we made our way through the woods, I dragged a pine bough behind, trying to blot out as much of our tracks as possible. Two big oxen left a really visible trail on the wet ground. Any fool could track us, I knew, and Liam Ratch was no fool.

I was out of breath and sore of foot when we finally came out of the woods on the edge of a broad farm field. The field sloped steeply to the edge of a rushing stream.

"That has to be Fish Creek," I said to John.

"Yes," he agreed. "Look, over that way." He pointed to the east. "I see the roof of General Schuyler's mill."

The field was dotted with shocks of wheat. I looked around the clearing and saw no sign of movement, no sign of Liam Ratch or his Indian friends. Thunder rumbled nearby. I prodded Goliath, and the oxen made their way down through the field, slipping and sliding on the wet ground. John sat up straight on Fred's back, his eyes roving from side to side watching for any sign of Liam Ratch.

Big raindrops began to pelt us. At the bottom of the hill was a stand of trees at the edge of a steep bank. It did not take much prodding to get Goliath and Fred trotting toward it. I ran along behind, mud clumps hitting me in the face from the oxen's hooves. It was hard to see, the rain was so heavy.

We crossed a narrow roadway that followed the line of the creek and came under the shelter of tall trees.

"Whoa!" I called to Goliath and Fred. Below us, at the bottom of a sheer drop, roared rain-swollen Fish Creek. The oxen seemed satisfied to huddle under the spread of a giant oak tree which afforded a little shelter from the downpour. I helped John slide down from Fred's back, and we sat against the base of the tree.

The wind whipped and thunder rumbled louder. Goliath and Fred turned their rumps to the wind and stood with their heads down. Suddenly a shadowy figure appeared through the wall of rain. Goliath snorted. The man hesitated for a moment, then walked right up to us and stood over us.

"Well, ain't this providence? Looks like I've found my missing oxen and my missing captives."

There was no mistaking the grating voice of Liam Ratch.

"So you sweet-talked my Lily into letting you go. Lily used to have better sense than to listen to conniving riffraff like you."

"She didn't let us go," I said lamely. "We got out of the cellar and ran for it while she was tending to Daisy and Rose and Gardenia."

Mr. Ratch towered over us. Water ran off the brim of his slouch hat and poured down on us.

"You wouldn't know the truth if it bit you," he snarled. "Never met a girl told more lies than you do."

"Please, Mr. Ratch, don't hurt Lily. She felt beholden to us for helping her."

"She should have felt beholden to her own pa who she owes her very life. Now get up, both of you. The British commissary is waiting for these oxen and that cartload of goods. The two braves who wanted to buy you didn't wait around, but I reckon I'll be able to deal you to somebody before the end of the day."

I got to my feet and gave John a hand up. He put his crutch under his arm to balance himself. Mr. Ratch snatched the prod from my hand and came alongside Fred.

Just then there was a brilliant flash and a deafening crack of thunder. It frightened Goliath and Fred so badly that they swung full about, bellowing. Goliath's broad rump hit Mr. Ratch and knocked him off balance. He tried to right himself, but the sodden clay soil was as slick as warm molasses. He slipped and slid right over the edge of the precipice and disappeared. I moved closer to the embankment. Mr. Ratch rolled and slid, bouncing off trees as he plummeted down the slope.

"Climb up, John!" I cried.

The trembling oxen were snorting and shifting their feet, but I was able to boost John back up onto Fred's back. Another clap of thunder sounded, not quite so close this time, and the rain grew lighter.

"Let's go!" I pulled on the end of the yoke, and we sloshed down the road. We were a ways from the Schuyler farm and mills still, although I could see the shingled roofs of the buildings through the trees. One way or another, we had to get across the swollen creek, and quickly. If Mr. Ratch managed to get out of the creek, he'd be waiting for us downstream.

We came to a place where the hillside was not so steep and the rapids did not appear to be so strong.

"Cross here, Annie," John called. "Don't take a chance on making it to the bridge. If he washed downstream, Mr. Ratch may be there."

I steered Goliath and Fred down to the water's edge.

"Come on, Goliath," I urged the big red ox. "We can make it."

I plunged into the rushing water. It was deeper than it had appeared, and the current was strong. I stayed on the upstream side of the team, next to Fred, clinging to the yoke. John lay flat on Fred's back, his arms wrapped around the animal's neck. Halfway across, I slipped on the rocks and was tossed under the roiling water. My hands slipped off the yoke and I was swept back, bouncing against Fred. I hit the rocky bottom and pushed with all my strength. My head popped up out of the water.

"Annie! Grab Fred's tail!"

I was tossed along Fred's side. Taking John's advice, I grabbed for the ox's tail, but I could not hold it. Desperately I reached out as the raging water swept me around the back of the team. As I whirled past them, the switch of Goliath's tail brushed against my face. I seized it with both hands. I was pulled underwater again as the oxen lunged forward. My lungs were near to bursting when I broke the surface, gasping for air. My feet touched bottom. I clung desperately to Goliath's tail, stumbling over the rocks as the oxen scrambled from the creek. They made their way up the slippery embankment, pulling me along behind. We had made it.

I let go of Goliath's sodden tail and slumped to the ground. Footsteps sloshed toward us, but I could not get up. I was too exhausted to run from Liam Ratch again. My chest ached and my legs throbbed. If I were destined to be sold to the Indians, so be it. I had run as far as I was able.

"Annie!"

Josiah knelt in the muck by my side and pulled me tight against him. Captain Landers and Mr. McGinnis helped John down from Fred's back.

"Mr. Ratch . . ." I gasped. "He's after us."

"Not any more, he's not," Josiah said. "By now he's swimming in the Hudson River. We saw him float past just before you went into the creek." Josiah pushed me back to arm's length and glared at me sternly.

"What you did was foolish. You could have been killed. And all for the sake of two dumb oxen."

"They're not so dumb, Josiah," I said. "They're the ones who knocked Mr. Ratch into the river."

CHAPTER 16–

Saturday, September 13, 1777

"Come along, Bella."

I led the cow out of the barn and down to the road. Ma waited for me there with a large bundle slung over her back and two crates of hens piled on a handcart. We had buried most of our household goods . . . pots and pans and tools and such. As sad as it made me to do that, to leave our home and all that was dear to me, burying those things gave me hope that we would come back. We would take only bedding and a few pots and spoons, sewing needles and clothing.

I looked up at the bluff behind our house. The log breastworks that General Kosciusko had ordered built loomed on the top of the hill. Josiah waved to me as he drove Goliath and Fred along the crest, a great log skidding behind them as they strained mightily, all their muscle and sinew pulling into the yoke. Goliath's sweaty red coat glistened in the bright sun. Mr. McGinnis doffed his hat and waved to me, too, as Henry and George labored right behind Goliath and Fred.

When John and I had returned to the farm with Goliath and Fred nearly three weeks past, Josiah told me that it was my choice whether or not to offer them to the patriot cause.

"You took such great risk to bring them back, Annie," he said, "I will not tell you that you must give them up. They are yours to do with as you choose."

I had stood between Goliath and Fred, stroking their broad heads. "Are the Continentals truly going to build fortifications up there?" I asked, pointing up to the hill behind our house.

"Yes," he had answered.

"Then you must take them."

If my brother believed so strongly in the cause of independence, if he was going to help build the fortifications that would stop the British advance down our valley, I surely wanted him to have a good ox team to work with. Josiah, Ma and me and our oxen would give all we had to give in this war.

The Tranes had gone. Nathaniel and Julia were afraid for their newborn daughter's safety, so they traveled down to Albany, where Julia's father had settled on a new farm in the hills just south of the city. All the settlers in the valley were fearful of the danger to come. Very few had not already packed up and moved into the villages. Nathaniel and Julia had pleaded with us to go with them.

At first, Ma insisted that I take their offer and go along with them.

"Why must I go?" I'd asked. "Why are you not going too?"

"I may be needed here, Annie," she'd said softly, taking both my hands in hers.

I was not able to hide my dismay. For months, I had listened to all this talk of war, and it seemed like it would never happen, it was just talk. I really wasn't sure just what war was. Men in fine uniforms marching in straight lines, fifes whistling, drums beating, sunlight on polished bayonets and gun barrels. That is what we saw in the village. It was exciting.

But I knew in my heart that when the war came, it would not be exciting. Men would die. Homes would burn. Horses would die, too, and oxen. Lives would change forever. War was a dark cloud hanging over the sunlit valley of the Hudson, even uglier and more threatening than the thunderstorms that had beset us for the whole month of August. And I knew why Ma would be needed.

"I will not go," I'd said, standing up as straight and tall as I could. "I can help, too. With all these soldiers and militia coming into camp, there is much work to do. I can cook and mend and tend livestock."

To my surprise, after a time, Ma had agreed. We were going to take Bella and some bedding and food and settle in with the militia and other families near Stillwater. John was already there with his father. Mrs. McGinnis and her three daughters had gone out to the valley of the Mohawk River, to the settlement called Schenectada to stay with her sister's family, but John had persuaded his father to let him stay to help take care of the horses and oxen. He was getting along very well with his crutch, excited to be able to do his part, too.

For the past week, more and more soldiers had been coming in. Six hundred New Hampshiremen just two days ago. The army and militia had dug in near the village. By all reckoning, General Gates now commanded an army of more than ten thousand men. With the fortifications now being built as Josiah had predicted, right there on the bluff looking over our farm, we were squarely in the path of any battle that was to come.

Just after sunup this morning, Captain Landers had stopped by our house.

"The British and Germans broke camp at Fort Miller three days ago," he told us. "They're moving our way . . . men, horses, artillery, baggage and hundreds of camp followers. There is no turning back now."

So Ma and I had packed up what we could carry, buried the rest and crated up the hens we had left. We would move, as our neighbors had, to what we hoped would be a safer place.

"We're ready, Ma," I said, tugging on Bella's lead rope. She was more interested in grazing alongside the road than in walking to the encampment.

We walked briskly in the brilliant September afternoon. The sky was as blue as a sky could be, and bright sunshine bathed the fields and woods. Here and there, splashes of scarlet and gold touched the trees, hinting at autumn soon to be upon us.

Above us on the hilltop, the ring of axes sounded as the men felled trees for more breastworks. Preparations for battle were all around us . . . a battle that no one wanted, but that everyone knew was coming as sure as the winter was coming. The British could wait no longer.

As I trudged alongside Ma, I thought that I must be feeling as Liam Ratch felt when he was swept along in the rushing waters of Fish Creek . . . like there was no way to stop, no way to turn back. It was as though we were all being carried helplessly along in floodwaters, not knowing where it would take us, or if we would survive.

I thought about Lily and her sisters, caught somewhere maybe even closer to the war than we were. Lily had lost her mother, her home, and perhaps even her father, no-account as he was. And if the massed army and militia of the colonies were able to stop General Burgoyne and his troops, she would lose her country, too.

I took one last look back, but I could no longer see Josiah or Goliath and Fred. All I could see was the sun-washed woods and the serene river. The rhythmic plod of Bella's hooves, the clatter of the handcart and the chirp of birds lulled us as we walked.

We rounded a bend in the road, and coming toward us at quick time was a large force of Continental soldiers and militia, their muskets shouldered, their faces grim. We stood aside as they passed by us on the road. Most of the men tipped their hats or nodded to us. In a few moments, the entire group had gone on out of sight, hurrying north to meet the enemy.

"It's coming, Annie," Ma said, a tremor in her voice. "It will start soon."

I fingered the cat's claw necklace that Gardenia had given me so I could run as fast as a catamount, and I shivered. There would be no more running. The time to stand and fight was at hand.

October 18, 1777

The face of defeat was grimy and weary. I stood near the road in front of our house in the mid-afternoon sun watching as the surrendered forces of General Burgoyne's army trudged past. They were sullen and silent. I offered them water from the spring which they gratefully accepted, tipping their hats and murmuring their thanks as they moved on.

"They will be ferried across the river at Vandenburgh's Crossing," Josiah had told us that morning as he turned Goliath and Fred out in the pasture behind our barn. "General Gates promised them they'll be sent back to their own countries."

It had been a great victory, but hard-won, the men in the camp said. They had made their stand, stood together and stopped the mighty British and German armies. They were proud, and so was I.

During the two weeks the armies faced each other across redoubts and ravines, I had stayed behind at the camp with John, mending and cooking and tending livestock. Ma was called to tend to the wounded men, and spent long hours away, sometimes not coming back to camp for several days. She said little of what she did or saw in the makeshift battlefront hospital, but each night I heard her softly weeping in her bed.

Josiah had not gotten into the thick of the fighting, for which I was thankful. His company of men were stationed on the hill near our house, ready to fight if the enemy broke through at the Great

Ravine and moved south along the river. That never happened. The main forces of Continental soldiers and militia stood their ground gamely and repelled the British attack at John Freeman's farm. Then both sides dug in and waited, skirmishing occasionally, until finally on October 7, General Burgoyne had tried a desperate push through our Continental lines. A fierce battle at Mr. Barber's field showed him that we were a force to be reckoned with. The next day, the British and Germans had fled north to the village of Saratoga.

Captain Landers told us that General Stark, the hero of Bennington, cut off their route of retreat when he and his men fortified a rocky hill above the village and bottled up the British and Germans. Surrounded and with nowhere to go, General Burgoyne had finally given up, surrendering to General Gates on October 17.

It was a bright but cool and sunny day. The enemy soldiers marched by our house throughout the morning into the afternoon, the camp followers straggling along after them. Josiah and Mr. McGinnis had gone down to Stillwater to help keep order as the retreat continued. John had been allowed to go along, and he was very excited.

"We are calling them 'troops of convention'" Josiah had told Ma with a laugh. "They say they have not surrendered, just agreed to go home and fight no more."

"Surrendered or not surrendered," Ma had said, "I'm glad they're done fighting, and I'm glad they're going. And I am glad to be back home."

I was glad to be home, too, glad the fighting was over. We had dug up our household tools and dishes and tried to act as if all was as it had been, as if none of the horror of the past few weeks had happened. But standing by the side of the road, watching the dispirited enemy pass by, it was impossible to pretend that none of it had happened.

As the solemn-faced Germans in their worn, dirty uniforms disappeared down the road, the last group, the German women and children, along with their small herd of livestock, gathered around the spring. I dipped another pail of water and handed the dipper to the first one in line, an older woman, stooped and grey-haired.

"*Danke schoen*," she said, touching my arm with soiled, blistered hands.

"You are welcome," I replied.

"Annie?"

A small, ragged girl pushed her way to the front of the line.

"Gardenia!" I knelt down and embraced the frail child. "Where is Lily? How did you get here?"

Gardenia turned around. A tall blonde woman with a red-cheeked baby balanced on her left hip stepped through the cluster of women.

"This is Olga," Gardenia said, "and her baby is Anton. I help take care of Anton."

I nodded to Olga. "But where is Lily?" I repeated.

"Gone to Canada," Gardenia replied.

"Why didn't you go with her?"

"Papa says I am too slow, and the wilderness is too dangerous for slow children. No one would sell him any horses, so they set out on foot. Papa left me at the camp. He said the women would care for me."

"He left you with strangers?" I could not believe that even Liam Ratch could be heartless enough to abandon his own child.

"Lily came to me the night they left," Olga said. "She cried as if her heart would break. She gave me two gold pieces and pleaded with me to look out for Gardenia."

Gardenia leaned in close to me, and whispered in my ear. "I don't want to go to Braunschweig, Annie."

I looked into Gardenia's serious dark eyes. I knew from what Josiah had said that the defeated troops and their camp followers would walk overland to Boston, a hard journey that would take weeks in weather that was rapidly turning colder. With her twisted foot, how would Gardenia keep up?

The women who had already drunk from the bucket slung their bundles over their shoulders and headed down the road. I refilled the pail and set it before the next woman in line.

"It seems that you have enough of a burden with Anton," I said to Olga. "Even though you promised Lily you would take care of Gardenia, I know that Lily would not mind if you left her here with us."

Olga shifted Anton to her other hip. "Times are very hard," she said.

"I know that."

"The journey will be difficult."

I nodded.

"The child seems to care for you."

"As I care for her."

Tears welled in Olga's eyes. "I have become fond of her. And she has been such a help with Anton."

"Please," I said. "Let her stay. It is hard for her to walk great distances."

Olga reached out her hand and stroked Gardenia's hair. "We will miss you, *das blumlein*," she said in a voice barely more than a whisper.

Gardenia clung tightly to my hand as we watched Olga turn and trudge down the muddy road after the other women. She looked up at me and smiled, and I hugged her close to me.

"Your necklace did save my life, Gardenia," I said, slipping the cat's claw necklace over my head and laying it around her neck. "I give it back to you now so you will never again be too slow to run from danger."

From the pasture up on the hill, Goliath let out a lusty moo.

"Come with me," I said. "We will bring Goliath and Fred down to the barn."

"So no one will steal them?"

I smiled. "So no one will steal them."

I thought back to the night of the Full Red Moon when Liam Ratch had stolen them. How all of our lives had changed since that night just two months past. I took the hand of Liam Ratch's daughter and together we walked up the hill to get Goliath and Fred.

* * * * * * * * * * * * * * * * *

AUTHOR'S NOTE:

I am forever grateful to gentle giants Clem and Briggs and their owners, Pat Guilmette and Ken Plummer, for showing us the story's heart, and to Erika Kemble, Maya DeMarco, Ryan McBride and Sam DeCelle for bringing the characters to life.

BIBLIOGRAPHY:

1. <u>Saratoga: Turning Point of America's Revolution</u> by Richard Ketchum, Henry Holt & Co, 1997

2. <u>Burgoyne's Campaign</u> by Charles Neilson, J. Munsell, 1844

3. <u>In the Path of War: Children of the American Revolution Tell Their Stories</u>, edited by Jeanne Winston Adler, Cobblestone Publishing Co, 1998

4. <u>Our County and Its People</u>, pub 1898

5. <u>In Praise of Oxen</u> by Terry James, 1992

Printed in the United States
141803LV00002B/4/P

9 781598 588781